Accounting for Healthcare

In an era where digital transformation is revolutionising every sector, the healthcare industry stands at a significant crossroad. With Value-Based Healthcare (VBHC) at the core of this transition, the role of accountants is evolving dramatically. This book brings these pieces together to guide accountants and interested readers through the changing landscape.

The book begins by demystifying VBHC and introducing the concept of digital health. It examines how the digital transition is impacting accountants in the healthcare sector, outlining their shifting roles from traditional data processors to strategic advisors. The chapters delve into a broad range of topics including performance evaluation, operational budgeting, capital investment, and the need for adaptability in dealing with technological advancements. Alongside this, it showcases how these changes are shaping the future of accounting in healthcare and the skills necessary to navigate these novel pathways.

Targeted primarily at accountants, financial professionals in healthcare and health sector leaders, this book also serves as an accessible guide for those new to the subject. The readers will gain a comprehensive understanding of the intersection of healthcare, accounting and digital technology, appreciating the value that adept accountants can bring to the VBHC journey. The book comes complete with real-world case studies, illuminating the complexities and rewards of VBHC's digital transition. Additionally, it includes supplementary materials to further enrich understanding, including a glossary of terms and online resources to explore the topics in depth.

Gillian Vesty is a Professor and Deputy Dean L&T in the School of Accounting, Information Systems and Supply Chain at RMIT University, Melbourne, Australia. She is a member of CPA Australia, a board member of the Institute of Management Accountants, Australia and New Zealand and teaches in the field of management accounting.

Miia Jansson is an Adjunct Professor of nursing science at the University of Oulu, Finland. She is also an adjunct associate professor in the STEM College at RMIT University, Melbourne, Australia.

Tarek Rana is an Associate Professor of accounting in the School of Accounting, Information Systems and Supply Chain at RMIT University, Melbourne, Australia. His research spans various aspects of accounting and management. His works focus on accounting and management control, public sector management, risk management, resilience, sustainability, and the intersection of technology with accounting practices. He has contributed to understanding risk management and management control systems, particularly in the public sector, and the role of accounting for sustainability.

Kerryn Butler-Henderson is a Professor and Director of the RMIT Digital Health Hub at RMIT University. She is a well-respected digital health academic, with more than 20 years of experience working in health and higher education.

Routledge Studies in Accounting

4. **Strategic Pricing and Management Accounting**
   David Dugdale

5. **Statutory Audits in Europe**
   Latest Reforms and Future Challenges
   Michael Kend, Giulia Leoni, Cristina Florio and Silvia Gaia

6. **The Privatisation of British Rail**
   How Not to Run a Railway
   Sean McCartney and John Stittle

7. **The UK Accounting Standards Board, 1990–2000**
   Restoring Honesty and Trust in Accounting
   David Tweedie, Allan Cook and Geoffrey Whittington

8. **Auditing Transformation**
   Regulation, Digitalisation and Sustainability
   Edited by Jan Marton, Fredrik Nilsson and Peter Öhman

9. **Integrated Reporting and Performance Measurement Systems**
   Bogusława Bek-Gaik and Anna Surowiec

10. **Financial Reporting for Islamic Financial Institutions**
    Accounting Standards, Interpretation and Application
    Abdul Rauf Mahar, Ayesha Bhatti, Muhammad Junaid Ashraf and Asfand Zubair Malik

11. **Accounting for Healthcare**
    The Digital Transition to Value-Based Healthcare
    Edited by Gillian Vesty, Miia Jansson, Tarek Rana and Kerryn Butler-Henderson

For more information about this series, please visit www.routledge.com/Routledge-Studies-in-Accounting/book-series/SE0715

Accounting for Healthcare

The Digital Transition to Value-Based Healthcare

Edited by Gillian Vesty, Miia Jansson, Tarek Rana and Kerryn Butler-Henderson

Routledge
Taylor & Francis Group
LONDON AND NEW YORK

First published 2024
by Routledge
4 Park Square, Milton Park, Abingdon, Oxon OX14 4RN

and by Routledge
605 Third Avenue, New York, NY 10158

Routledge is an imprint of the Taylor & Francis Group, an informa business

British Library Cataloguing-in-Publication Data
A catalogue record for this book is available from the British Library

Library of Congress Cataloguing-in-Publication Data
Names: Vesty, Gillian, editor.
Title: Accounting for healthcare : the digital transition to value-based healthcare / edited by Gillian Vesty, Miia Jansson, Tarek Rana and Kerryn Butler-Henderson.
Description: 1 Edition. | New York, NY : Routledge, 2024. | Series: Routledge studies in accounting | Includes bibliographical references and index.
Identifiers: LCCN 2023052409 (print) | LCCN 2023052410 (ebook) | ISBN 9781032685380 (hardback) | ISBN 9781032685472 (paperback) | ISBN 9781032685489 (ebook)
Subjects: LCSH: Health facilities--Accounting. | Managerial accounting. | Accounting--Computer programs. | Accounting--Data processing.
Classification: LCC HF5686.H7 A33 2024 (print) | LCC HF5686.H7 (ebook) | DDC 362.1068/1--dc23/eng/20231109
LC record available at https://lccn.loc.gov/2023052409
LC ebook record available at https://lccn.loc.gov/2023052410

ISBN: 978-1-032-68538-0 (hbk)
ISBN: 978-1-032-68547-2 (pbk)
ISBN: 978-1-032-68548-9 (ebk)

DOI: 10.4324/9781032685489

Typeset in Sabon
by MPS Limited, Dehradun

Gillian Vesty dedicates this book to her husband Haydn and family, who have continually provided support through her nursing and academic careers. In addition, the ongoing support from Roger Wale and healthcare colleagues has been invaluable in bringing to life the challenges faced in this sector.

Miia Jansson dedicates this book to her husband Jussi, along with Oulu University, who has provided mentorship and supported her important international research collaborations.

Tarek Rana dedicates this book to Professor Lee Parker, a great mentor and esteemed colleague, and to the memory of late Professor Kerry Jacobs, his inspirational Ph.D. supervisor, whose guidance and wisdom have been invaluable.

Kerryn Butler-Henderson dedicates this book to Professor Kathleen Gray, mentor, workforce and education visionary and long-time friend.

Contents

Editors Biographies

Gillian Vesty is a professor and Deputy Dean L&T in the School of Accounting, Information Systems and Supply Chain at RMIT University, Melbourne, Australia. She is a member of CPA Australia, a board member of the Institute of Management Accountants, Australia and New Zealand and teaches in the field of management accounting. Prior to becoming an academic, Gillian worked in the healthcare sector as a registered nurse. She has worked in hospitals throughout Australia and the United Kingdom. Her research interests seek to align management accounting's performance evaluation and strategic budgeting with social impact research that addresses health and wellbeing challenges from a value-based healthcare perspective. She is also an active board member of Games for Change, Asia Pacific, fostering the nexus between simulated artefacts in the form of serious games to provide a powerful vehicle for ongoing experimental research. Gillian is on the editorial board of *Accounting Auditing and Accountability Journal.*

Miia Jansson is an adjunct professor of nursing science at the University of Oulu, Finland. She is also an adjunct associate professor in the STEM College at RMIT University, Melbourne, Australia. Her research interests are in the areas of digitalisation and value-based healthcare with a focus on the impact of digital health. Her publications span journal articles, book chapters, edited books, and editorials. Her publications have appeared in prestigious high-ranking journals such as *International Journal of Medical Informatics, BMC Health Services Research, Games for Health Journal, Journal of Advanced Nursing, Journal of Clinical Journal of Telemedicine and Telecare,* and *Meditari Accountancy Research*. Further to her academic contributions, Dr Jansson is an experienced PhD researcher with a strong practical nursing science background.

Tarek Rana is an associate professor of accounting in the School of Accounting, Information Systems and Supply Chain at RMIT University, Melbourne, Australia. He teaches management accounting, forensic business investigation and data analytics. His research interests are in the areas of digitalisation, strategic management, management control systems, performance measurement, risk management and sustainability, with focus on the healthcare, not-for-profit and public sector organisations. His publications span journal articles, book chapters, edited books, research monographs and editorials. His publications appeared in reputable accounting, management and interdisciplinary journals such as *Accounting Auditing and Accountability Journal, The British Accounting Review, Intelligent Systems in Accounting Finance & Management, Financial Accountability & Management, Qualitative Research in Accounting and Management, Meditari Accountancy Research, Business Strategy and the Environment, Public Money & Management, Journal of Accounting & Organisational Change, Journal of Cleaner Production,* and *Journal of Intellectual Capital.* Further to his academic contributions, Dr Rana is a Chartered Accountant and Chartered Management Accountant and brings a professional record of accomplishment including partnership in accounting firms, board membership and governance experience as both executive and non-executive director.

Kerryn Butler-Henderson is a professor and director of the RMIT Digital Health Hub at RMIT University. She is a well-respected digital health academic, with more than 20 years of experience working in health and higher education. She is known for her passion and dedication to the promotion and advocacy of the digital health workforce and involved with several large, funded research projects evaluating digital health interventions in various health settings. Kerryn is a fellow of the Australasian Institute of Digital Health (AIDH) and Deputy Editor of the *BMJ Health and Care Informatics* journal. She was recognised for her expertise in 2021 as a Future50 Health IT Leader by HIMSS and 2022 as a Telstra Health Brilliant Women of Digital Health Award recipient.

Figures

Tables

Contributors

Salma Arabi is a PhD candidate in the School of Health and Biomedical Sciences at RMIT University, Australia. She holds a Bachelor of Applied Science in Exercise and Sport Science. She is also a first-class honours graduate, graduating with a Bachelor of Health and Biomedical Sciences (Honours). Salma has been listed on the RMIT Vice-Chancellor's List for Academic Excellence where she graduated in the top 2% of all graduates in 2020. Salma is currently completing her PhD where she will be exploring collaborative partnerships in healthcare using a distributed leadership approach.

Kerryn Butler-Henderson is a professor and director of the RMIT Digital Health Hub at RMIT University. She is a well-respected digital health academic, with more than 20 years' experience working in health and higher education. She is known for her passion and dedication to the promotion and advocacy of the digital health workforce and involved with several large, funded research projects evaluating digital health interventions in various health settings. Kerryn is a Fellow of the Australasian Institute of Digital Health (AIDH) and Deputy Editor on the BMJ Health and Care Informatics journal. She was recognised for her expertise in 2021 as a Future50 Health IT Leader by HIMSS and 2022 as a Telstra Health Brilliant Women of Digital Health Award recipient.

Kanika Dhamija is a higher education lecturer in accounting and economics at Trinity College, University of Melbourne. She holds a Bachelor of Economics degree and completed master in professional accounting. Currently she is enrolled in PhD in accounting at RMIT University, Australia. She is also an Associate Member of CPA Australia and an Academic Member of IPA, Australia. She is a firm believer in the transformative power of education and has dedicated the last seven years to teaching and mentoring students, nurturing their intellectual growth in accounting and economics subjects. Kanika's current research is centred around Public Hospitals, Healthcare, Value-based Care, Management Accounting, Performance Measurement and Patient-centred Care.

Malshika Dias is a lecturer in information systems at the College of Business and Law, RMIT University. She received her PhD from the University of New South Wales (UNSW Sydney). Malshika's research interests lie at the intersection of technology, strategy and organisation, focusing on various forms of information systems. She has expertise in qualitative research methods, in particular, case study research and historical narrativist approaches. Dr Dias's work has appeared in the *Journal of Strategic Information Systems* (JSIS). She has presented numerous research papers at international conferences, including the International Conference on Information Systems (ICIS), European Conference on Information Systems (ECIS) and Pacific Asia Conference on Information Systems (PACIS).

Miia Jansson is an adjunct professor of nursing science at the University of Oulu, Finland. She is also an adjunct associate professor in the STEM College at RMIT University, Melbourne, Australia. Her research interests are in the areas of digitalisation and value-based healthcare with a focus on the impact of digital health. Her publications span journal articles, book chapters, edited books and editorials. Her publications have appeared in prestigious high-ranking journals such as *International Journal of Medical Informatics, BMC Health Services Research, Games for Health Journal, Journal of Advanced Nursing, Journal of Clinical Journal of Telemedicine and Telecare* and *Meditari Accountancy Research*. Further to her academic contributions, Dr Jansson is an experienced PhD researcher with a strong practical nursing science background.

Vijayajothy Jayakumar is a senior lecturer in accounting at the University of Peradeniya, Sri Lanka, and currently a lecturer at Peter Faber Business School, Australian Catholic University. She holds a BSc in Accounting and an MBA and received her PhD in Accounting from RMIT University, Australia. She is also an associate member of the Chartered Institute of Management Accountants (UK) and the Chartered Global Management Accountant. She is a recipient of the People's Choice Award 2021 in the 3 Minute Thesis (3MT) competition at the College of Business and Law, RMIT University, Australia. Dr Vijayajothy's current research and teaching interests are centred around NFP business models, aged care and health care performance measurement, accounting, management accounting and management control systems.

My T.N. Nguyen is a lecturer at the School of Haiphong University of Technology and Management, Vietnam, and currently works for RMIT University. She holds a PhD degree in supply chain and logistics from RMIT University (Australia), a Master of Science degree, and a Bachelor of Science degree from Vietnam Maritime University (Vietnam). Dr My's pursuit of an academic career stemmed from her passion for education, and her current research and teaching interests are maritime supply chain, maritime risk management and healthcare supply chain management.

Shams Rahman is a professor at the Department of Supply Chain and Logistics, RMIT University, Australia, who in 2021, has been recognised among the world's top 2% scholars. Professor Rahman has served in executive and leadership positions for several universities in research and innovation and has advised multinational companies and consulting firms on lean manufacturing, remanufacturing, sustainability, food cold chain and talent management and successfully led several externally funded projects. Professor Rahman is an associate editor of the *International Journal of Information Systems and Supply Chain Management* and sits on the editorial board of 15 international journals. He has published over 245 research papers and served as a guest editor for several top-ranked journals. Professor Rahman is dedicated to interdisciplinary research and education and integrated approaches to defining and unravelling supply chain challenges and societal concerns. His current research interest is in supply chain sustainability and disruptive technology and talent management.

Tarek Rana is an associate professor of accounting in the School of Accounting, Information Systems and Supply Chain at RMIT University, Melbourne, Australia. He teaches management accounting, forensic business investigation and data analytics. His research interests are in the areas of digitalisation, strategic management, management control systems, performance measurement, risk management and sustainability, with focus on the healthcare, not-for-profit and public sector organisations. His publications span journal articles, book chapters, edited books, research monographs and editorials. His publications appeared in reputable accounting, management and interdisciplinary journals such as *Accounting Auditing and Accountability Journal, The British Accounting Review, Intelligent Systems in Accounting, Finance & Management, Financial Accountability & Management, Qualitative Research in Accounting and Management, Meditari Accountancy Research, Business Strategy and the Environment, Public Money & Management, Journal of Accounting & Organisational Change, Journal of Cleaner Production and Journal of Intellectual Capital.* Further to his academic contributions, Dr Rana is chartered accountant and chartered management accountant and brings a professional record of accomplishment including partnership in accounting firms, board membership and governance experience as both executive and non-executive directors.

Say Yen Teoh is a senior lecturer and researcher at RMIT University and serves in the Department of Information Systems and Business Analytics. She specialises in digital technologies, blockchain and enterprise systems research. Having earned her PhD from the National University of Singapore, she has expanded her research internationally, forging collaborations with industries in Australia, China, Malaysia, Singapore, Thailand and the United States. Say Yen actively bridges the gap between theoretical knowledge and real-world applications. Her engagement with industry stakeholders translates academic insights into practical solutions that positively influence business and society. She published in esteemed journals, including *Information Systems Journal*, *Communications of AIS* and *Information Technology & People*. Say Yen's approach exemplifies a unique blend of scholarly excellence and practical applicability, contributing meaningfully to academia and industry.

Vinh Thai is a professor of logistics and supply chain management at the School of Accounting, Information Systems and Supply Chain of RMIT University in Melbourne, Australia, and also the founder of the Australian Maritime Logistics Research Network (AMLRN). Professor Thai is an active academic with experience both in the industry and academia, with teaching, research and higher-degree research supervision in the broad areas of supply chain and maritime logistics management. Professor Thai is currently an associate editor of the *Asian Journal of Shipping and Logistics* and has published widely in top-tier international academic journals such as *Transportation Research Part A: Policy & Practice*, *Transportation Research Part E: Logistics & Transportation Review*, *International Journal of Logistics Management*, *Marine Policy*, *Maritime Policy & Management*, *Maritime Economics and Logistics*, etc., as well as industry periodicals such as Daily Cargo News. His expert opinion has also appeared in various sources of media. He has been consulting on projects for ASEAN Secretariat, Japan International Cooperation Agency (JICA), World Bank in Vietnam and World Bank in Indonesia. He has also been invited to speak or participate as a panelist at many international academic and industry conferences and seminars, including at international organisations such as the OECD.

Gillian Vesty is a professor and deputy dean L&T in the School of Accounting, Information Systems and Supply Chain at RMIT University, Melbourne, Australia. She is a member of CPA Australia, a board member of the Institute of Management Accountants, Australia and New Zealand and teaches in the field of management accounting. Prior to becoming an academic, Gillian worked in the healthcare sector as a registered nurse. She has worked in hospitals throughout Australia and the UK. Her research interests seek to align management accounting's performance evaluation and strategic budgeting with social impact research that address health and well-being challenges from a value-based healthcare perspective. She is also an active board member of Games for Change, Asia Pacific, fostering the nexus between simulated artefacts in the form of serious games to provide a powerful vehicle for ongoing experimental research. Gillian is on the editorial board of *Accounting Auditing and Accountability Journal*.

Foreword

This research book provides insights into Australia's changing healthcare landscape. Healthcare is an important contributor to the national economy, with spending on healthcare accounting for more than 10% of gross domestic product (GDP). In the wake of the COVID-19 pandemic, the healthcare system experienced an unprecedented crisis in clinical staffing levels and bottlenecks in service delivery. This book provides insights into the emerging new healthcare economy and the concept of value-based healthcare (VBHC) which is now emerging as an important part of Australia's as well as global healthcare strategy. It offers new knowledge and information to accountants and healthcare managers on the hybridised skills required, across budgeting and performance evaluation, to enhance the accounting profession's contribution to the delivery of VBHC. Through a series of case study chapters, this book offers a future-focused lens on the changes underway in healthcare delivery and the hybridisation of accounting expertise required. Interviews with multidisciplinary actors in the healthcare field provide insight into future skills requirements for accountants. Details of the impact of digital transformations in healthcare, and new incentives from governments to improve patient access and quality of care, are examined in light of changing investment appraisal and new notions associated with VBHC ideals. As modes of delivery shift to deal with hospital bed blocks and capitalise on digital innovations, resourcing an expanding Hospital in the Home (HITH) concept is also considered from an accounting perspective. While this book is directed towards accounting and healthcare professionals and considers the implications for accounting in the move towards VBHC in Australia, it nonetheless provides a useful resource for all clinical and administrative workforce, including students seeking employment in varying roles within the healthcare sector. It also provides a research agenda, with many insights uncovered in this study still requiring further investigation. With health economics driving big-picture changes, there is a lack of understanding of how economic models are impacting at an operational level. Research to date tends to be from a clinical perspective, and there is less data available from an accounting, performance measurement and budgeting perspective. With VBHC still emerging and the digital explosion in its infancy, there are opportunities to continue to explore the unfolding changes in funding, investment, procurement, budgeting, management control, risk management and performance evaluation.

Chapter Synopses

The first chapter provides an overview of the study, which commences with the underlying value-driven literature that supports the investigation. An outline of the research methodology – a qualitative field study approach, comprising interviews with experts throughout Australia and one in Finland – provides a comparative basis on which to benchmark the ways in which VBHC has influenced performance evaluation and budgeting in this country. The chapter concludes with a summary of the key takeaways from each of the topic areas covered in this book.

The second chapter provides a comprehensive overview of VBHC, the key literature in the area and the efforts to measure outcomes. Insights from field interviews demonstrate that VBHC is actioned in Australia under the quadruple aim of improving the patient experience, improving the health of populations and improving the provider experience while overall reducing the costs of care. This chapter considers the non-financial performance indicators that support the measurement of improvements in experience and population health. The challenges faced by providers are discussed, with key takeaways for accounting including insights into the hybridised skills required to transition Australia's healthcare system to a value-based approach.

The third chapter provides an overview of healthcare system budgeting and financial flows across the sector. While the focus is on the public healthcare system and hospital activity-based funding (ABF) models, it is acknowledged that this is changing due to advances in technology and digitisation, whereby patients may be monitored and treated remotely and beyond the walls of the hospital. While the ABF model is based on health economic modelling, the operational activities in terms of performance evaluation and budgeting tend to be hidden in the academic literature. This domain is largely the role of the management or strategic management accountant. Increasingly, this role has the potential to contribute to the value chain of activities across the sector, with a likely expansion in the scope of the management accountant role. Issues with the funding models are explored, with a focus on how accounting can support, from a financial performance measurement perspective, both operational and capital expenditure in VBHC.

The fourth chapter comprises details of health information system flows across the sector. Challenges with current systems are discussed, along with emerging technologies that have the capacity to transform healthcare delivery, cost management and resource allocation. This chapter provides insights on the health information systems and the staged rollout of electronic medical records (EMRs), which will drive rapid escalation of cloud-based information sharing and artificial intelligence (AI)-based predictive modelling, to support administrative and clinical decision-making. These insights help to understand the accounting interventions that can support improvements in the system efficiency and aid in performance evaluation for operational and strategic decision-making.

The fifth chapter contributes to understanding the emerging trend towards population health and resourcing community healthcare needs. With a focus on supply chain management for remote healthcare and HITH, this case study examines the procurement activities that can help accountants understand the value chain activities that are being conducted both within and outside the hospital walls. The significant takeaway from this study is the gradual move to break down the barriers between primary and hospital healthcare provision. With this change, there are new insights from a supply chain management perspective.

The sixth chapter revisits key themes related to workforce upskilling for VBHC and circles back to the hybridising expertise and current requirements for workforce upskilling. It underscores the importance of enhancing competencies across the workforce, not only in accounting but also in strategic planning, budgeting, and performance measurement from diverse financial and non-financial perspectives. To thid end, this chapter provides a comprehensive discussion on the criticality of upskilling for effective engagement in these areas.

The seventh chapter concludes the book and provides further reflections and extensions on the key emergent themes and outlines future research directions. It introduces new perspectives not fully explored within the book, aiming to develop future research work and academic scholarship in the context of VBHC, investment in digital health, the changing roles of accountants, and the interplay between management control, performance measurement and risk management, suggesting these areas will remain relevant and significant for years ahead.

Acknowledgements

This book is the product of a research project funded by CPA Australia as part of their Global Research Perspective Program. The authors would like to thank CPA Australia for funding this research. They would also like to thank the interview participants for their valuable time and important contributions.

Acknowledgments

[illegible]

1 Hybridising Accounting Expertise

Gillian Vesty, Miia Jansson, Tarek Rana, and Kerryn Butler-Henderson

1.1 Introduction

For some decades, public healthcare has been faced with a key challenge – how to combat rising costs at the same time as meeting universal access ideals. Against this backdrop, the COVID-19 pandemic revealed not only unprecedented clinical staffing shortfalls and bottlenecks in service delivery, it also gave rise to greater public value and expectations globally. The emergence of digital innovations and analytics offers new possibilities for public health service delivery. However, these technological solutions and their business models do not align with existing funding models, which results in resource allocation issues and system stagnation. Understanding the emergence of the new healthcare economy, through interviews with experts in the field, can provide accounting professionals with the knowledge and hybridised skills necessary to enhance their contribution to innovative new healthcare delivery models.

Value-based healthcare (VBHC) is a healthcare delivery model in which providers, including hospitals and physicians, are paid based on patient health outcomes. The 'value' in VBHC is derived from measuring health outcomes against the cost of delivering the outcomes (Teisberg et al., 2020). Maximising value is the central idea of VBHC and is broadly measured in the following value equation:

$$\frac{Outcomes}{Costs} = Value$$

The equation comprises 'costs' which are all the expenditure items associated with treating a patient with a given condition, or diagnosis-related group (DRG), while 'outcomes' are what matters most to patients (Porter and Teisberg, 2006). Thus, this formula ensures the patient's priorities take precedence by drawing attention to the delivery of quality care while minimising costs for that care. The VBHC movement in Australia is not necessarily framed under the label 'value-based healthcare' but follows the **quadruple aim** – i.e., improve patient experience, improve population health,

DOI: 10.4324/9781032685489-1

reduce cost of care and improve provider experience (Iglesia et al., 2020). It is this quadruple aim which is driving healthcare delivery quality improvements and changes to resource allocation.

Through a series of case study chapters, this book provides a future-focused lens on the changes occurring in healthcare delivery, which are impacting performance evaluation, budgeting and overall resource allocation, in order to transform patient access and quality of care. These six chapters explore the notion of VBHC, activity-based funding (ABF) and resource allocation in public hospitals, along with the impacts of digital health on strategic management and performance measurement within the sector. The insights presented in each chapter are informed by field interviews with multidisciplinary experts, who offer valuable perspectives on the hybridised skills and expertise required to effectively and efficiently support VBHC advancement.

1.2 Problem Identification

The healthcare sector in Australia, like other parts of the world particuarly in the Organisation for Economic Co-operation and Development (OECD) countries, is excited by the implications of delivering world-class VBHC. In Australia **VBHC** is defined as 'a sustainable health system that delivers outcomes that matter to patients and the community, is personalised, invests in wellness and is digitally enabled' (NSW Health, 2021). Inspired by the early work of Porter and Teisberg (2006) and extended by Teisberg et al. (2020), this global movement is transformed by key enablers: measurement and evaluation, digital health and analytics and funding and purchasing – concepts which shift the focus from activity to outcomes. As demonstrated throughout this research book, there are tensions between current government ABF models and the need to shift to a 'value-based' model, where VBHC strategies embed the ideals of the quadruple aim (Vesty et al., 2022). To support accountants in understanding this significant change in the healthcare sector, the strategic approach proposed by Teisberg et al. (2020) has been adapted by Vesty et al. (2022) and is detailed in Table 1.1.

In line with this emerging 'value-based' model, the international group Leapfrog to Value (Maru et al., 2019, p. 5) has outlined three core principles of **measure, deliver** and **pay,** as shown in Figure 1.1.

According to the Leapfrog report, nations can adopt value-based care to help achieve universal access to healthcare services. They argue that governments and donors can take the following actions. First, they can cultivate experimentation with value-based care models. Second, they can apply a value lens to near-term decisions that have long-term implications. Third, they can establish an enabling environment for value-based care models to scale and position countries to 'leapfrog to value'.

To achieve value in healthcare, it is important to prioritise efficient outcomes, high-quality information for all stakeholders and consideration of the broader context of disease, while leveraging digital innovation in

Table 1.1 Strategic framework for VBHC implementation

Strategy	*How can accountants support?*
Understand the shared health needs of patients	Support VBHC move and provide insights into the resource trade-offs and benefits (reconfiguring cost structures to focus on the immediate health needs of patients while simultaneously understanding and managing costs).
Design solutions to improve health outcomes	Guide clinician innovators with enhanced cost-benefit modelling of their time-limited digital health interventions that sit outside the ABF model.
Integrate learning teams	Be part of the journey in terms of assessing staffing impacts, digital health investments and enhancing workforce technological capacity.
Measure health outcomes and costs	Perform digital health investment appraisal and performance measurement that aligns with VBHC objectives.
Expand partnerships	Accounting has the means to build new accounting networks with systems that extend ABF to VBHC measures and further incentivise the 'system', so the population benefits from distributed arrangements.

Note

Adapted from 'Accounting, valuing and investing in healthcare: Dealing with outdated accounting models' by Vesty, G. M., Kokshagina, O., Jansson, M., Cheong, F., & Butler-Henderson, K., 2022, *Meditari Accountancy Research*, *31*(1), 52–77 (https://doi-org.ezproxy.lib.rmit.edu.au/10.1108/MEDAR-06-2021-1334). Copyright © 2022 by Emerald Publishing Limited.

evaluation. Care can be improved by prioritising equitable accessibility, affordability, safety, continuity of care and patient-centeredness.

Value measurement requires the following four approaches: **outcome perceptions, data aggregation, data standardisation** and acknowledgement of medical, social, environmental and behavioural causes of disease in **performance evaluation.** Care delivery is built from carefully designed patient care pathways, management learning feedback loops and balancing primary, tertiary and preventative care. Furthermore, Maru et al. (2019) emphasise the importance of health system priorities in payment system design that improve access to care, by understanding how and where care is delivered and shaped by resource flows. With the understanding that access to care benefits everyone, it is essential to experiment and adapt payment model to fit local contexts. We build on these concepts in this book and extend them to include the Australian context. Taking a future-focused management accounting for value approach, we consider **measure** in terms of accounting financial and non-financial performance metrics; **deliver** in terms of managing a future-focused value-added healthcare supply chain; and **pay** in terms of operational budgeting, capital budgeting and strategic investment. A future-focused approach necessitates a digital health overlay and consideration of the role of artificial intelligence (AI) along with demand planning for delivering care beyond the hospital walls.

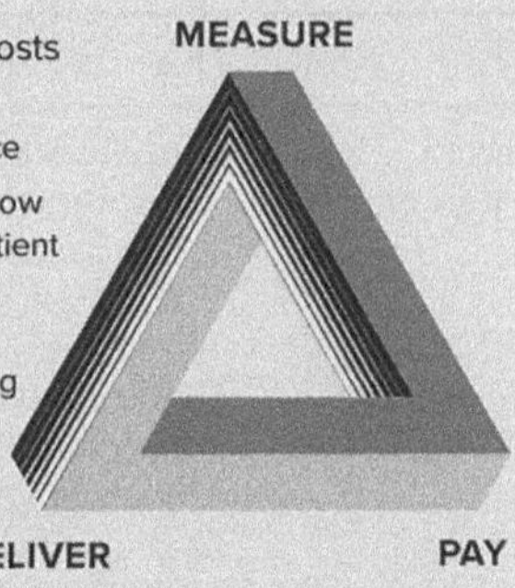

MEASURE value in terms of outcomes and costs

1 Track outcomes that matter to patients: clinical outcomes, quality of life, and patient experience
2 Aggregate data longitudinally, to understand how costs and outcomes accrue throughout the patient journey
3 Make data insightful and actionable by standardizing, benchmarking, and risk-adjusting
4 Integrate medical and non-biomedical data (social, environmental, behavioral) to understand the root causes of disease

DELIVER value by using data to learn and improve performance

1 Design care pathways around the patient journey
2 Establish iterative loops of learning and improvement that involve frontline providers and senior decision-makers
3 Emphasize preventive care in community and primary care settings when possible, providing access to hospital-based treatment when necessary

PAY for value to incentivize continued improvement

1 Provide transparency for providers into outcomes and cost data, and move away from volume-based payments that promote unnecessary care
2 Design payment models that reward the highest value care
3 Reward caring for the sickest and most remote to ensure all patients benefit from value-based care

Figure 1.1 Leapfrog to Value: Measure, Deliver and Pay.

Note: Adapted from "Leapfrog to Value: How nations can adopt value-based care on the path to universal health coverage" by Maru, C., Lin, A., Kagubare, K., Pollack, A., Stern, A., Rao, N., & Walker, J., 2019, p. 5 (https://static1.squarespace.com/static/5db772d44638535b2114f2e6/t/5ddea52751c72e2c5edacd77/1574872363413/2019_LeapfrogToValue.pdf). Copyright © 2019 by Leapfrog to Value. Reprinted with permission.

This study aims to equip hospital accountants, and managers, with the essential hybridised expertise required in a healthcare sector that has been radically changed by the COVID-19 pandemic. It is increasingly important to manage effective supply chain of healthcare service delivery to ensure an uninterrupted delivery of value to the end-user, which might mean remote monitoring, telehealth and/or discharge to Hospital in the Home (HITH), managed by a multidisciplinary team of experts. Existing incentivised funding models are slow to shift the allocation of resources to population health ideals and rather than streamlining, add further complexity to the system. While still far from meeting utopian ideals, from a management accounting and control perspective, the **design, delivery, costing** and **pricing** of value-based care requires new expertise and innovative insights. A move towards VBHC requires accountants who possess hybrid skills and the ability to work with clinical complexities, initiate qualitative performance metrics and alternative drivers of hospital income and cash flows that support digital health investment appraisal and assist in financing different visions of the healthcare value chain.

Our key research question for this case-based project is:

What hybrid skills should hospital accountants be equipped with for enhanced support and employability in the move to value-based healthcare?

To explore this question, interviews are held with multidisciplinary experts from the field to provide alternative insights of skills requirements. The underpinning theory is drawn from sociology and is used to better understand the justifications of management that align with their different interpretations of value. This is discussed in the following section.

1.3 Theoretical Framework

The economies of worth framework (Boltanski and Thévenot, 2006) helps to identify and define 'value' in the healthcare setting. From interviews in the field, this framework can support new ways of measuring value and/or new ways of using existing data to support performance evaluation of VBHC improvements.

In their work Boltanski and Thévenot (2006) argue that justification and critique rely on different orders of worth, each of which operationalise distinct guiding principles. Based on extensive observation as well as seminal bodies of literature, Boltanski and Thévenot (2006, 1999) identify six justificatory regimes or worlds of worth in societies (see Table 1.1). The **market world** exists when the value of competition and rivalry are taken into consideration and guide decisions of managers. Whereas the **industrial world** finds its legitimacy and longevity of business is affected through an efficiency principle. Meanwhile, the **civic world** is deemed worthy when formal rules and regulatory processes are followed and believed to be the highest principle in society. The worthiness of the **domestic world** emerges when institutional actors honour the value of tradition, familiarity and hierarchy in organisational justifications and decisions. The **inspired world** perspective places value on innovation and 'inspiration', upheld as the higher-order position. The final sixth world order is the **world of fame** or opinion in which public or popular opinion counts and being 'famous' is valued as the highest principle. The orders of worth are not limited to six classifications but evolve over time. For instance, further to these initial orders, Thévenot et al. (2000) introduce a **green** order of worth, a world with emphasis on caring for ecosystems and nurturing the important value of being an environmentally friendly society.

Each of the orders of the worth is characterised through unique criteria that defines their position within the group of worlds. The criteria are used by managers and comprise the **mode of evaluation** or **worth**. For example, price in the market world or efficiency in the industrial world. An order of worth is justified through a **test**, such as measures of market effectiveness (i.e., return on investment) or trustworthiness in the domestic order of worth. Justification is also motivated by providing a **form of relevant proof,** such as monetary gain in market world or measurable statistics in the industrial world. It is important to identify the **qualified objects** in each of the distinct orders of worth as these will be used in debate and exemplified by the **qualified human beings** who are brought in for their expert opinion to help sway the argument in distinct ways. Each order of worth is designated by its distinct **time formation** and **space formation** (Thévenot et al., 2000). For example, in the world of opinion/fame, the standard for evaluation can be tested through how popular a person is or whether this individual is widely recognised and has a widespread audience.

This world is populated by celebrities – as qualified human beings/objects – who gain their popularity through media as an object. The proof of this world is usually done through semiotic ways, but the popularity highly depends on the trend in time (time formation) and will end when trends change. Popularity is disseminated by means of communication network and thus celebrities are popular in their own network where they belong to (space formation). On the other hand, the market world is based on the competitive principle; the worthiness is tested on the degree of competition evaluated using means of costs or prices in monetary terms. The objects of this world are products or goods to sell for customers (qualified human beings). A schematic overview of the orders of the worth is presented in Table 1.2.

For this project, it is important to understand from the outset that coming to common agreement and agreeing on a particular point of view on operationalising VBHC in practice is not necessarily possible. Since each of the 'worlds' have their own standard for what is considered just or appropriate, the variations in legitimacy judgements between orders of worth can create disagreements and controversies (Boltanski and Thévenot, 2006). For example, when a leading pharmaceutical company releases a new drug or product under their name (qualified object), from the world of fame point of view it is possible that the more famous the company is, the greater the sales volume. Alternatively, a marketing manager taking a market world point of view, would argue that regardless of the popularity of the company, the quantity of products sold is determined by the ability to which the product can compete in the market. This is determined, for example, by the product quality, target customers and competitors. The same would apply to large commercial digital health organisations and the provisions of new digital health information systems or products to support VBHC initiatives.

This is due to the different logics or interpretations of measured worthiness, by different senior decision-makers (Smith-Lacroix et al., 2012). As a result, disharmony tends to emerge which can only be settled by compromise arrangements or agreeing to disagree and leaving the conflict unresolved (Boltanski and Thévenot, 2006). Under compromise arrangements, multiple orders of worth can co-exist through resorting to the common interest or common good (van Bommel, 2014). Multiple rationalities can affect the coordination of organisational activities with the settlement of conflicts

Table 1.2 Economies of worth framework

	Market	*Industrial*	*Civic*	*Domestic*	*Inspired*	*Fame*
Mode of evaluation	Price, cost	Technical efficiency	Collective welfare	Esteem, reputation	Grace, singularity, creativeness	Renown, fame
Test	Market competitiveness	Competence, reliability, planning	Equality and solidarity	Trustworthiness	Passion, enthusiasm	Popularity, audience, recognition
Form of relevant proof	Monetary	Measurable, criteria, statistics	Formal, official	Oral, exemplary, personal warranted	Emotional involvement & expression	Semiotic
Devalued characteristics	Defeat	Inefficiency, unproductivity	Individualism	Vulgarity, treachery	Habits, routines, realism	Indifference, disinterest
Qualified objects	Freely circulating market good or service	Infrastructure project, technical object, method, plan	Rules and regulations, fundamental rights, welfare policies	Patrimony, locale, heritage	Emotionally invested body or item: the sublime	Sign, media
Qualified human beings	Customer, consumer, merchant, seller	Engineer, professional, expert	Equal citizens, solidary unions	Authority	Creative being	Celebrity
Time formation	Short-term, flexibility	Long-term planned future	Perennial	Customary past	Eschatological, revolutionary, visionary moment	Vogue, trend
Space formation	Globalisation	Cartesian space	Detachment	Local, proximal anchoring	Presence	Communication network

Note

Adapted from "The more things change … Institutional maintenance as justification work in the credit rating industry" by Taupin, B., 2012, *M@n@gement,* (5), 529–562 (https://www.cairn.info/revue-management-2012-5-page-529.htm). & Adapted from "The Sociology of Critical Capacity" by Boltanski, L., & Thévenot, L., 1999, *European Journal of Social Theory,* 2(3), 359–377 (https://doi.org/10.1177/136843199002003010).

between the orders of worth and within a world of worth being central to the economies of worth thesis (Annisette and Richardson, 2011; Vesty et al., 2018).

This theoretical framework has been usefully applied to explore the justificatory responses of a range of managers in a French Government hospital when asked about the use of specific performance metrics (Morinière and Georgescu, 2022, p. 35). For example, the civic order of worth was explained in terms of universal coverage and 'principles of the equal right of access to care'. The industrial order of worth was described in terms of being a factory and a chain of production in meeting volume-driven output targets. The market order of worth was argued in terms of hospital profitability, whereas the domestic order of worth related to the hierarchy of staff who make decisions. Inspired order of worth in the French public hospital system was explained by a Deputy Director General in terms of: *our profession is transcendent because our actions are part of a bigger picture* (Morinière and Georgescu, 2022, p. 31). As imagined the sometimes-conflicting views result in performance measurement becoming a moral issue and one that continually needs compromise. This is particularly so between clinicians and administrators managing budgets and meeting patient demands. Van Elk et al. (2021) similarly identified that the management ideas of gurus, like Porter's VBHC, are adopted 'because their normative content can help otherwise divided organisations forge compromises. However, these compromises bring normative constraints and promote risk-aversion in turbulent times' (2021, p. 1). In the UK hospital under investigation in Van Elk et al., the authors noted that senior managers could justify the VBHC approach because they could adopt an 'outcomes' approach to managing performance. However, to do this everywhere for all admission treatment types was an impossibility. Hence, the justificatory decisions and compromise around measuring outcomes were left to only three patient treatment types. This then created an agenda for resourcing and new measurement ways to demonstrate worthiness of service provision in the move to VBHC.

Because VBHC is in its infancy in Australia, with different interpretations of 'value' in care delivery and some jurisdictions preferring a quadruple aim approach to improving health outcomes, the theoretical framework proposed by Boltanski and Thévenot (2006) provides a useful way to view the emergence of VBHC and an overall interpretation of dominant themes and compromise arrangements.

1.4 Interpretive Case Study Approach

To better understand the complex nature of the VBHC, we adopted an interpretive case study approach (Kakkuri-Knuuttila et al., 2008). This method is suitable for exploring ongoing flows of information when an in-depth study of an emerging phenomenon is needed (Pan and Tan, 2011; Walsham, 1995). To ensure confidentiality, we used pseudonyms for the names of all the participants and organisations and for any organisational-specific information systems. We sought to identify stakeholders in the Australian healthcare sector that could provide us with data relating to accounting, information flows and value-creation opportunities through digital health. The most important data sources were semi-structured interviews and publicly available data. We identified several stakeholders from the primary health networks for semi-structured interviews and other secondary data sources such as government reports and archival material.

Using qualitative content analysis techniques, we approached data analysis from an interpretive perspective (Corbin and Strauss, 2014). Throughout the analysis, we held regular team meetings to discuss and adapt our individual ideas towards building a collective analysis of the data in several stages. Our collective interpretations included the perspectives of the research team and feedback from our participations.

First, we read publicly available data, such as healthcare reports and stakeholder websites to obtain a broad overview of the research topic. The overview helped us revise our interview guide and to have an informed discussion with the interview participants. Second, we discussed our preliminary interviews among the team to understand their views on VBHC and how each of the perspectives under investigation – accounting, digital health, information systems and technologies, clinical and supply chain management – can support the operationalisation of VBHC in Australia. Third, we started analysing the interview data while still conducting the interviews to help build to data saturation and highlight areas that had been under-explored.

We coded interview transcripts, memos and field notes of the ongoing interviews. To allow source criticism, we triangulated the interview data with insights from publicly available data. While focusing on the phenomenon under study (i.e., the role of accounting in the move to VBHC), we retained 'a considerable degree of openness to the field data, and a willingness to modify initial assumptions and theories' (Walsham, 1995, p. 76), to ensure that we were not constrained in identifying new issues and insights. In each chapter, we provide a summary of the key findings before providing our interpretations in the findings section. The important take-away points are included at the end of each chapter.

1.4.1 *Interviewee Demographics*

Semi-structured interviews were held with policymakers, hospital managers from accounting, clinical coding, digital health, clinicians and commercial AI companies. The interviews were conducted with participants who have expertise in the Australian and Finnish healthcare fields, including recognised leaders in public sector health administration (see Table 1.3). Finland was selected as a comparative country, because of prior research collaborations and access to healthcare network support. One of the Finnish co-authors was able to spend time in Australia on research sabbatical to help with this study. Publicly available reports, including from Independent Hospital Pricing Authority

Table 1.3 Respondents with expertise from the field

Respondent	*Gender*	*Expertise*
1.	Male	General Practitioner
2.	Female	Hospital Health Information Systems, State Manager
3.	Female	Clinical Coder
4.	Female	Clinical Coder
5.	Male	Digital Start-up Company Co-founder
6.	Male	Accountant, Healthcare Service Provider
7.	Male	Health Technology Company, Software Engineer
8.	Male	Chief Executive, Digital Health Company
9.	Male	Chief Operating Officer, Digital Health Company
10.	Male	Chief Digital Health Officer
11.	Female	Hospital Manager – Clinician and Health Informatics
12.	Male	Health Department Administrator
13.	Male	Senior Executive, Government Funding Authority
14.	Male	Hospital in the Home, Medical Director and Physician
15.	Male	Accounting Executive
16.	Female	Accountant, Digital Start-up Company Co-founder
17.	Female	Hospital in the Home, Clinical Manager
18.	Male	Health Economist, Value-Based Healthcare Manager
19.	Male	Health Economist, Activity-Based Funding Advisor
20.	Male	Accountant and Health Department Administrator

(IHPA), along with other archival data were used to inform the research. The reports provided insights into the emerging accounting role in health and the public sector in terms of supply chain management, digital health and data analytics for improved performance evaluation and outcomes reporting.

Additional conversations on the preliminary findings helped to refine the case studies which will also be used for educational training and upskilling. The qualitative interview data and information from publicly available reports were used to craft distinct case studies in the following areas: operational budgeting, digital health investment and performance evaluation – all reflect the emerging move to VBHC and impacts to hospital funding and measurement of value. Importantly, each of the case studies will focus on the technology skills required by the hospital accountant. While the focus is on the public sector, interviews held with administrators and digital health start-ups from the private system provide further insights.

1.5 Outline of Chapters and Summary of Chapter Findings

The strategic VBHC framework adapted by Vesty et al. (2022) has guided the chapters that follow. The accounting focus, determined by interviewees, has resulted in the following structure and findings outlined in Table 1.4.

In the sections that follow, the problem being explored is discussed. This is followed by an overview of the underpinning sociological framework by Boltanski and Thévenot (2006) that helps explain the categories of value and ways in which management decisions and debates emerge from their

Table 1.4 Summary of chapter findings

Strategy	*Accounting focused findings*	*Insights from this study*
Understand the shared health needs of patients Measure health outcomes and costs	Detail current VBHC activities and **reconfigured structures** and provide insights into value-based non-financial **performance measurement** that understands the immediate health needs of patients.	Chapter 2
Measure health outcomes and costs Design solutions to improve health outcomes	Detail current **activity-based funding model** and **financial performance measurement** and how the costing systems align with VBHC objectives. Co-create with multidisciplinary innovators on the design and delivery of **accounting solutions** that meet VBHC objectives.	Chapter 3
Design solutions to improve health outcomes	Detail digital infrastructure **risk management, data flows** and **digital health investment** appraisal activities.	Chapter 4
Expand partnerships	Detail the emerging **value/supply chain management** system where the population benefits from **distributed hybrid care** arrangements, such as Hospital in the Home. Supply chain management for **integrated care** is essential in the move to VBHC.	Chapter 5
Integrate learning teams	Be part of the journey in terms of assessing workforce impacts, digital health investments and enhancing workforce technological capacity.	Chapter 6

different value propositions. Each chapter is a separate case study, outlining the different issues being experienced across the sector. The findings section in this chapter provides a summary of each of the key takeaways that culminate in the final chapter on upskilling the workforce.

The first case study in Chapter 2 provides a comprehensive overview of VBHC, the key literature in the area and the efforts to measure outcomes. Insights from interviews demonstrate that VBHC is actioned in Australia under the quadruple aim of improving the patient experience, improving the health of populations and improving the provider experience while overall reducing the costs of care. This chapter considers the non-financial performance indicators that support the measurement of improvements in experience and population health. The challenges faced by providers are discussed with key takeaways for accounting, including insights into the hybridised skills required to transition Australia's healthcare system to a value-based approach.

The second case study in Chapter 3 provides an overview of the healthcare system budgeting and financial flows across the sector. While the focus is the public healthcare system and hospital ABF models, it is acknowledged that this is changing due to advances in technology and digitisation, whereby patients may be monitored and treated remotely and beyond the wall of the hospital. Insights into how this system works are provided. Discussion on some of the issues emerging more recently because of pandemics and staff shortages, along with emerging trends and changes in the dynamics of healthcare delivery. While the ABF model is based on health economic modelling, the operational activities in terms of performance evaluation and budgeting tend to be hidden in the academic literature. This domain is largely the role of the management accountant and the potential to contribute to the value chain of activities across the sector is increasing, along with the scope of the role of the hospital management accountant. Interviews with multi-discipline actors in the field provide the basis for future skills requirements. These are further teased out in the case studies that follow.

The third case study in Chapter 4 comprises details of the information systems flows in the Australian hospital setting including data collected through electronic medical records and Hospital Information Systems. With its multifaceted role in healthcare, digital health therapeutics or interventions, such as patient monitoring, disease detection, prevention and management. Insights from interviews with health information systems managers and digital healthcare technology developers shed light on how these systems are measured and managed, the connections between systems and data and the possibilities and requirements for future system improvements. The study also identifies current system challenges, which can help to guide accounting interventions to support system improvements and ultimately facilitate performance evaluation for operational and strategic decision-making.

The fourth case study in Chapter 5 contributes to the emerging trend towards population health and resourcing community healthcare needs. With a focus on supply chain management for remote care and HITH, or hospitals without walls, this case study examines the procurement activities that can help accountants understand the value chain activities that are being conducted both within and outside the hospital walls. The significant takeaway from this study is the gradual move to break down the barriers between primary and hospital healthcare provision. With this change, there are new insights from a supply chain perspective.

The fifth and final case study in Chapter 6 circles back to the hybridising expertise and current requirements for workforce upskilling. This case not only draws attention to hybridising accounting expertise but also the rest of the workforce to better engage in planning, budgeting and performance evaluation from different financial and non-financial perspectives.

1.6 Conclusion and Key Takeaways

This chapter contributes to the broader conversation on the evolution of healthcare delivery models, the role of value in healthcare and the ways in which global challenges can be met through innovation, adaptation and a reimagined understanding of worth for a VBHC model. The contributions of this chapter are summarised below:

1. **Holistic Understanding of Public Healthcare's Challenges:** This chapter provides a comprehensive overview of the issues faced by global public healthcare, emphasising the complex interplay between rising costs, service delivery bottlenecks and clinical staffing shortfalls, particularly highlighted by the COVID-19 pandemic.
2. **Introduction to VBHC:** The chapter presents an in-depth discussion on VBHC as an evolving healthcare delivery model. It elucidates the core principle of the model – optimising patient outcomes relative to costs.
3. **Australian Perspective:** By shedding light on the unique adoption of VBHC in Australia, the chapter contributes insights into how different countries and regions might approach and adapt and contextualised the model based on local needs and objectives.
4. **Insights from Experts:** Drawing from field data, the chapter provides first-hand perspectives from multidisciplinary experts on the future of healthcare delivery and the hybrid skills essential for the progression of VBHC.
5. **Value Measurement Techniques:** The chapter breaks down the multi-faceted approaches to value measurement, encompassing outcome perceptions, data aggregation, standardisation and the integration of diverse determinants of health.
6. **Discussion on Digital Transformation:** Offering a forward-looking lens, the chapter underlines the significant roles digital health, AI and demand planning can play in redefining healthcare delivery beyond traditional settings.
7. **Economies of Worth Framework:** The chapter introduces readers to the economies of worth framework, highlighting how various orders of worth can help redefine and measure value in healthcare. This framework offers a novel approach to assessing healthcare improvements from a value perspective.
8. **Deep Dive into Orders of Worth:** By detailing the different orders of worth and their unique criteria, guiding principles and modes of evaluation, the chapter offers a comprehensive guide to understanding societal values and their application in the healthcare context.
9. **Connecting Theory and Practice:** Through detailed case studies and practical examples, the chapter bridges the gap between theoretical concepts and their real-world applications, ensuring readers can see the tangible impacts of the discussed concepts.
10. **Emphasis on Flexibility and Adaptation:** The chapter concludes with a new contribution to the discourse on the necessity of experimenting and adapting payment and healthcare delivery models to suit different local contexts, emphasising the importance of customisation in healthcare transformation.

In conclusion, as presented in Table 1.5, we have a summary of key takeaways from each chapter to support upskilling and hybridised accounting expertise. The overarching insights suggest that the funding models are drivers of activity with disparate roles within the system working to improve efficiencies and effectiveness on the margins of an outdated system, without collectively questioning how the system itself can be radically changed (Table 1.5).

Table 1.5 Summary of key takeaways

Chapter 1: Hybridising Accounting Expertise
Key Takeaway 1: The need for a strategic framework to support accountants in VBHC implementation.
Key Takeaway 2: The use of economies of worth framework to better understand value in healthcare settings.
Key Takeaway 3: The need to explore the challenges in understanding and operationalising VBHC.
Chapter 2: Accounting Impacts of Value-Based Healthcare
Key Takeaway 1: Understanding what matters to patients themselves is fundamental to improving healthcare. Accountants can support in the standardisation of outcome measures that matter to patients for improved management and evidence for value-based payment.
Key Takeaway 2: Multiple stakeholder perspectives need to be considered when developing and deploying value metrics for individual patient care pathways and scaling VBHC pilots in areas of chronic disease management. Accounting should play an important co-producer role, particularly in budgeting for new VBHC structures.
Key Takeaway 3: Education is required to ensure long-term budgeting and investment for VBHC change, and addressing this conflict can improve the provider experience.
Key Takeaway 4: There is a need to develop data analysis and visualisation tools to integrate data into clinical workflows to guide clinical decision-making. In addition, emerging AI and machine-learning techniques require accountants to embrace patient-reported outcome measures to predict outcomes and associated costs.
Key Takeaway 5: VBHC implementation requires resourcing strategy and uniformity across Australia. All technical, logistical, social and organisational barriers (e.g., workflow configuration, incentives and state/territory-based initiatives) need to be solved for improved alignment. Addressing this conflict would help to enhance the provider experience.
Chapter 3: Activity-Based Funding and Investment Appraisal
Key Takeaway 1: Have a detailed understanding of the costs and revenue streams to provide strategic insights.
Key Takeaway 2: Support investment appraisal in digital health with well-executed risk management strategies that do not stifle innovation. Consider incentives that support greater investment by insurers, pharma and other aligned organisations.
Key Takeaway 3: Be prepared to engage in extensive AI predictive analytics for clinical forecasting and cost management activities.

(*Continued*)

Table 1.5 (Continued)

Key Takeaway 4: Work on partnerships that foster accounting as a proactive co-producer of change.

Chapter 4: Health Information Systems in Value-Based Healthcare

Key Takeaway 1: Health information systems from various healthcare providers should be designed and implemented in a way to streamline workflows between different stakeholders in the healthcare ecosystem. To do so, the systems need to have necessary integration mechanisms in place from the planning stages.

Key Takeaway 2: Privacy and security-related issues on information sharing should be addressed through appropriate governance structures, mechanisms and policies. To do so, cyber security oversight is required to define user roles, access levels and other procedures along and across the data flows.

Key Takeaway 3: Open IT literacy should be improved across all healthcare industry stakeholder groups, from surgeons to general practitioners, to nurses, accounting and administration staff. To do so, education and training workshops need to be organised aiming to upskill staff on IT skills, privacy, cybersecurity and ethical concerns, as well on innovative applications (see Chapter 6 on Workforce Upskilling for Value-Based Healthcare).

Key Takeaway 4: Investing in emerging technologies should be considered when innovating for the future of the healthcare industry. Recent advancements such as AI and robotics open new avenues for providing VBHC. To do so, technology providers and healthcare stakeholders need to build better relationships and work together in the long-term, with accounting leading valuation and appraisal.

Chapter 5: Moving the Value Chain to Support Integrated Care

Key Takeaway 1: From a supply chain and logistics management perspective, virtual care and in-person care needs to be balanced and managed. There are multiple factors that impact standardisation of delivery which impact value-chain costs.

Key Takeaway 2: Accounting can support with insights into the impacts of changes in budgeting across the healthcare value chain including resourcing and procurement.

Key Takeaway 3: Accounting can support with enhanced cost of quality measures across the healthcare value chain by linking patient outcome measures to resourcing and procurement.

Chapter 6: Workforce Upskilling for Value-Based Healthcare

Key Takeaway 1: Accountants need skills to act as a **business co-producer** in providing a strong advisory and supporting role in leading innovative change, by recognising trends and opportunities as well as managing risk.

Key Takeaway 2: Accountants need to move more into being a **data navigator and transformer** using analytics and visualisations for strategic deep-dives and innovative insights on performance outcomes, for more streamlined and efficient operations that extend traditional boundaries.

Key Takeaway 3: While performance reporting is a given requirement, it is argued that digitally enhanced **audit and assurance** will provide greater support to clinical managers, particularly if enhanced with AI.

Key Takeaway 4: Accountants can be champions of **sustainability,** in developing investment appraisal and budgeting frameworks that support the achievement of Sustainable Development Goals (SDGs) from a population health and wellbeing perspective to sustainable resourcing.

References

Annisette, M., & Richardson, A. J. (2011). Justification and accounting: Applying sociology of worth to accounting research. *Accounting, Auditing & Accountability Journal*, 24(2), 229–249. 10.1108/09513571111100690

Boltanski, L., & Thévenot, L. (1999). The sociology of critical capacity. *European Journal of Social Theory*, 2(3), 359–377. 10.1177/136843199002003010

Boltanski, L., & Thévenot, L. (2006). *On justification: Economies of worth* (Vol. 27). Princeton University Press.

Corbin, J. & Strauss, A. (2014) *Basics of qualitative research* (3rd Ed.). Sage Publications.

Iglesia, E. G. A., Greenhawt, M., & Shaker, M. S. (2020). Achieving the quadruple aim to deliver value-based allergy care in an ever-evolving healthcare system. *Annals of Allergy, Asthma & Immunology*, *125*(2), 126–366. 10.1016/j.anai.2020.04.007

Kakkuri-Knuuttila, M. L., Lukka, K., & Kuorikoski, J (2008). Straddling between paradigms: A naturalistic philosophical case study on interpretive research in management accounting. *Accounting, Organizations and Society*, 33, 267–291.

Maru, C., Lin, A., Kagubare, K., Pollack, A., Stern, A., Rao, N., & Walker, J. (2019). *Leapfrog to Value: How nations can adopt value-based care on the path to universal health coverage*. Leapfrog to Value. https://static1.squarespace.com/static/5db772d44638535b2114f2e6/t/5ddea52751c72e2c5edacd77/1574872363413/2019_LeapfrogToValue.pdf

Morinière, A., & Georgescu, I. (2022). Hybridity and the use of performance measurement: Facilitating compromises of creating moral struggles? Insights from healthcare organizations. *Accounting, Auditing and Accountability Journal*, *35*(3), 801–829. 10.1108.AAAJ-12-2019-4309

NSW Health. (2021). *Value based healthcare in NSW*. NSW Government. https://www.health.nsw.gov.au/Value/Pages/value-based-healthcare-in-nsw.aspx#:~:text=A%20sustainable%20health%20system%20that,experiences%20of%20receiving%20care

Pan, S. L., & Tan, B. (2011). Demystifying case research: A structured–pragmatic–situational (SPS) approach to conducting case studies. *Information and Organization*, *21*(3), 161–176. 10.1016/j.infoandorg.2011.07.001

Porter, M. E., & Teisberg, E. O. (2006). *Redefining health care: Creating value-based competition on results*. Harvard Business Press.

Smith-Lacroix, J.-H., Durocher, S., & Gendron, Y. (2012). The erosion of jurisdiction: Auditing in a market value accounting regime. *Critical Perspectives on Accounting*, *23*(1), 36–53. 10.1016/j.cpa.2011.09.002

Teisberg, E., Wallace, S., & O'Hara, S. (2020). Defining and implementing value-based health care: A strategic framework. *Academic Medicine*, *95*(5), 682. 10.1097/ACM.0000000000003122

Thévenot, L., Moody, M., & Lafaye, C. (2000). Forms of valuing nature: Arguments and modes of justification in French and American environmental disputes. In M. Lamont & L. Thévenot (Eds.), *Rethinking comparative cultural sociology: Repertoires of evaluation in France and the United States* (pp. 229–272). Cambridge University Press. 10.1017/CBO9780511628108.009

van Bommel, K. (2014). Towards a legitimate compromise? An exploration of integrated reporting in the Netherlands. *Accounting, Auditing & Accountability Journal*, 27(7), 1157–1189. 10.1108/AAAJ-04-2013-1309

van Elk, S., Trenholm, S., Lee, R. H., & Ferlie, E. (2021). Adopting management philosophies: Management gurus, public organizations, and the economies of worth. *Public Management Review*, 124. 10.1080/14719037.2021.2014165
Vesty, G. M., Kokshagina, O., Jansson, M., Cheong, F., & Butler-Henderson, K. (2022). Accounting, valuing and investing in health care: Dealing with outdated accounting models. *Meditari Accountancy Research*, *31*(1), 52–77. https://doi-org.ezproxy.lib.rmit.edu.au/10.1108/MEDAR-06-2021-1334
Vesty, G. M., Ren., C., & Ji, S. (2018). Integrating reporting as a test of worth: A conversation with the chairman of an integrated reporting pilot organisation. *Accounting, Auditing and Accountability Journal*, *31*(5), 1406–1434. 10.1108/AAAJ-08-2016-2684
Walsham, G. (1995). Interpretive case studies in IS research: Nature and method. *European Journal of Information Systems*, 4(2), 74–81. 10.1057/ejis.1995.9

2 Accounting Impacts of Value-Based Healthcare

Gillian Vesty, Miia Jansson, Tarek Rana, Kerryn Butler-Henderson, and Kanika Dhamija

2.1 Introduction

This chapter introduces the notion of value-based healthcare (VBHC) and its impact and explores the notion of 'value' expressed by discipline experts in the field. In the following sections, VBHC literature is introduced and its impact on accounting and hybridised expertise is examined, including a discussion of the challenges and opportunities that arise with this shift in mindset. Evidence from interviews help to problematise the issue, which is then followed by discussion and implications for practice. The conclusion and overarching takeaways from this chapter are further explored in the chapters that follow.

2.2 Value-Based Healthcare

Porter and Teisberg (2006) introduced the VBHC strategy for how healthcare should be delivered and measured. Since then, healthcare systems around the world followed this value-driven approach to varying degrees. According to Porter (2009), prioritising value for patients is the primary strategy for addressing healthcare challenges, which involves measuring health outcomes achieved relative to the amount of money spent.

VBHC is a healthcare delivery model in which providers, including hospitals and physicians, are paid based on patient health outcomes. The 'value' in VBHC is derived from measuring health outcomes against the cost of delivering the outcomes (Teisberg et al., 2020). Maximising 'value' is the central ideal in VBHC and is broadly measured in the following value equation:

$$\frac{Outcomes}{Costs} = Value$$

The equation comprises 'costs' which are all the expenditure items associated with treating a patient with a given condition, or diagnosis-related group (DRG), and 'outcomes' are what matters most to patients (Porter and Teisberg, 2006). Thus, this formula ensures the patient's priorities take precedence by drawing attention to the delivery of quality care while

DOI: 10.4324/9781032685489-2

minimising costs for that care. With value defined as health outcomes achieved per dollar spent, value can be increased by lowering healthcare costs or improving outcomes, or both. As will be discussed in the following chapters, this perspective takes a long-term view. It's important to note that any short-term gains achieved by cost-cutting and reduced investment in health can ultimately erode perceptions of value, and poor investments in health can lead to a decline in outcomes over time, as is the case with dysfunctional behaviour when return on investment (ROI) is used as a short-term reward-based performance metric.

Putera (2017) further contends that the idea of VBHC is in line with patient-centred care. This approach humanises people rather than treating health as a commodity. Andersson et al. (2015) describe three guiding principles for implementing VBHC: focus on what creates value for patients, organise patient care around their medical conditions and complete care cycles and measure medical outcomes by improving the health of the population and cost efficiency.

Under value-based care agreements, providers are rewarded for helping patients improve their health, reduce the effects and incidence of chronic disease and live healthier lives in an evidence-based way. Researchers have identified benefits of adopting a VBHC approach, such as reduction in length of stay (Ahluwalia et al., 2019, 2021; Featherall et al., 2019; Lichkus et al., 2019); increased patient satisfaction (Ahluwalia et al., 2021; van Veghel et al., 2020a, 2020b); decrease in episode of care cost (Douglas et al., 2016; Featherall et al., 2019); reduction in total medical expenditure reimbursement (Miao et al., 2019); and increase in quality of life (quality-adjusted life years) (Goretti et al., 2020; Montesinos Gálvez et al., 2020).

Together this results in VBHC's quadruple aim: **improving patient experience, improving health of populations, reducing cost of care** and **improving provider experience** (Iglesia et al., 2020) which has become the guiding principle for a VBHC approach. This is also outlined in Table 2.1. Note that investment in integrated systems and digital health technology is crucial to achieving these goals and implicit in the benefits outlined in Table 2.1.

Table 2.1 Value-based healthcare benefits

Patients	*Providers*	*Payers*	*Suppliers*	*Society*
Lower costs	Higher patient satisfaction rates Affordability	Stronger cost controls, reduced duplications	Alignment of prices with patient outcomes	Reduced healthcare spending
Better outcomes	Better care Equitable access Efficiencies	Reduced risks		Better overall health

Note

Adapted from 'What is value-based healthcare' by NEJM Catalyst, 2017 (https://catalyst.nejm.org/doi/full/10.1056/CAT.17.0558). Copyright © 2017 by Massachusetts Medical Society.

2.2.1 Measuring 'Value' in Value-Based Healthcare

Nevertheless, it has been argued that to date, that the definition of 'value' in VBHC still lacks clarity, which is a significant methodological issue for researchers in the field (Mkanta et al., 2016). Even the Expert Panel of the European Commission on public health notes that there is no universal definition of 'value' within VBHC. While the term 'value-based healthcare' is increasingly used in public discourse, and 'value' is often understood as health outcomes relative to monetised inputs, the definition of 'value' is subjective, and opinions about what is valuable can differ among patients, clinicians, healthcare providers, policymakers and industry stakeholders (Duckett et al., 2008). Patient perceptions of value will in part depend on their expectations, which will be shaped by many personal factors (Zeithaml et al., 1990). A patient's perspective will include some, or all, of the following factors (Duckett, 2019, p. 18):

- Outcomes of care measured in clinical terms, such as complication rates.
- Outcomes of care measured in terms of the patient's assessment, such as relief of pain, ability to do lifestyle or job-related tasks that they would normally undertake. For example, mobility measures are important for orthopaedic surgery patients, or ability to do needlework is a measure used for patients offered eye procedures (Lundström and Pesudovs, 2009).
- Patient experience of care, such as being treated with dignity, privacy, the nature of staff interactions, cultural appropriateness, information provision and continuity of care.
- Issues associated with access to care, such as waiting times.
- Cost of care to the patient.

From a patient perspective, value outcomes need to be reasonable for their age and health condition. Hence some form of **adjusted value** expectations needs to be interpreted in the definition. According to Duckett, 'some people will be surgery averse and place a high weight on advice and reassurance, whereas others will be very concerned about out-of-pocket costs, and patients will vary according to pain tolerance. This heterogeneity of patient perspectives is one of the reasons it is difficult to translate the value-based, patient-oriented hype into meaningful policy' (2019, p. 18).

Gray (2015) provides further insights into value as three distinct categories: **allocative value** (fair distribution of resources to maximise value for the entire population), **technical value** (improvements in the quality and safety of healthcare delivery) and **personalised value** (individual patient values in combination with the best evidence and assessment of the patient's condition). With **societal value** being added to the list through the contribution of healthcare to social participation and connectedness, this comprehensive meaning of 'value' offers a wider perspective than the interpretation of 'value' as purely monetary in the context of cost-effectiveness.

Although the momentum has begun to shift in healthcare delivery systems from volume-driven, fragmented care to value-driven, coordinated care, as well as a transition in payment systems from fee-for-service models to comprehensive care payment systems (Miller, 2009), it is extremely gradual and incremental in design. As an ideal approach, VBHC is operationalised into six components that are assumed to be mutually reinforcing:

- Organise care into integrated practice units (IPUs).
- Measure outcomes and costs for every patient.
- Move to bundled payments for care cycles.
- Integrate care delivery across separate facilities.
- Expand excellent services across geography.
- Build an enabling information technology platform.

VBHC costs are not only those experienced from the provider perspective. Patients also spend less in managing their own treatment costs when care is organised as an integrated package. Over time as population health improves through prevention-based patient services, less time will be spent on chronic disease management, such as heart disease, chronic obstructive pulmonary disease, diabetes and/or cancer. Patients experience fewer doctor visits, medical tests, medications, hospital admissions and procedures, as health improves. Providers are rewarded for achieving value-based outcomes which further incentivises investment in prevention-based services. When payments are bundled to cover a full cycle of care (even for extended periods of a year or more) efficiency will be increased. Furthermore, linking procurement to VBHC initiatives, such as individualised therapies, will help recognise opportunities for efficiencies across the supply chain. At a societal level, the balancing act underpinning VBHC is indicated as an ROI model and depicted in Figure 2.1.

Investing in enabling information technology platforms such as electronic medical records (EMRs) creates a space for fostering integrated care – that is, primary care, speciality care and acute hospital care is all integrated in a single delivery model. The patient's primary doctor is expected to direct this total care package. VBHC takes a long view – considering value not based on

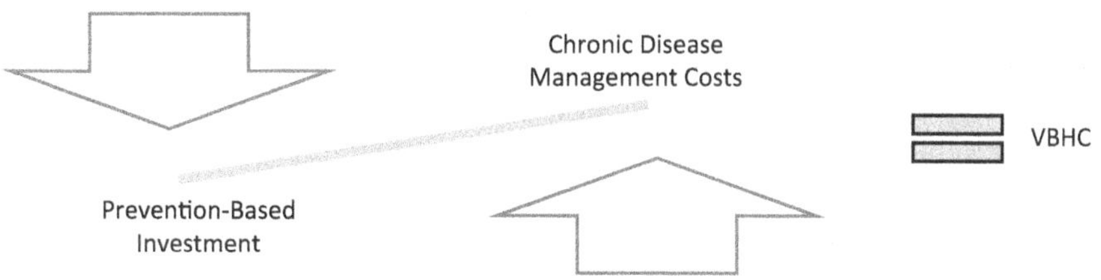

Figure 2.1 Balancing Returns on VBHC Investment.

a single healthcare encounter but in terms of the outcomes of a full pathway of care and the resources involved along the way.

VBHC also takes a system view: instead of asking an individual clinician to work harder or do better to improve care, it looks at how all aspects of a health system can enable better value in care delivery. In a VBHC system:

- **Patients:** Have their needs addressed in an integrated way.
- **Clinicians:** Have the data they need to continuously improve care.
- **Organisations:** Have incentives that are aligned with value for patients.

This integrated approach to health services delivery arguably 'strengthens people-centred health systems through the promotion of the comprehensive delivery of quality services across the life-course, designed according to the multidimensional needs of the population and the individual and delivered by a coordinated multidisciplinary team of providers working across settings and levels of care' (World Health Organization [WHO], 2020).

2.2.2 *Value-Based Healthcare Accounting Techniques and Non-financial Patient-Reported Outcomes*

Previous studies have taken extended accounting approaches to measure VBHC. For instance, scholars have noted that time-driven activity-based costing can help hospitals obtain more accurate cost information, better understanding of waste in the system for improved strategic decisions (for example, Kaplan, 2020; Kurt et al., 2019). This approach also supports environmental sustainability goals as well.

A number of international organisations have been formed to promote value-based care and improve healthcare quality globally. These include the International Consortium for Health Outcomes Measurement (ICHOM), the Patient-Reported Outcomes Tools, Engaging Users and Stakeholders (PROTEUS) Consortium, the Patient-Reported Outcomes Measurement Information System (PROMIS) and the PROMIS Health Organisation. Specifically, their missions are to improve health outcomes by developing, maintaining, improving and encouraging patients, clinicians and researchers to apply patient-reported outcomes (PROs) in clinical practice and clinical research. An example is shown in Table 2.2.

According to the PROTEUS Consortium, PROs are patients' own reports of how they feel, function, live their lives and survive. PROs can include generic and/or disease-specific questionnaires related to symptoms (e.g., pain, fatigue, nausea and depressive mood), functioning (e.g., activities of daily living and cognitive functioning) and/or quality of life (e.g., mental, physical and social well-being). When correctly measured, analysed and described, PROs could provide important insights into patient outcomes for guiding and improving care.

Table 2.2 Example of patient-centred outcome measures in chronic disease management

Disease/ condition	*Outcome*	*Measures*	*Reporting source*	*Timing*
Hip and knee osteoarthritis	Acute complications of treatment	Mortality	Clinical	30 days post-procedure
		Readmissions	Clinical	Continuous
	Patient-reported health status	Pain	PRO: NPR 0 – 10	Baseline, annually
		Physical functioning	PRO: HOOS-PS /KOOS-PS	
		Work status	PRO	
		HRQoL	PRO: EQ-5D-3L, SF-12 or VR-12	
		Overall satisfaction	PRO	
	Disease control	Reoperation or revision	Clinical	Continuous
		Need for surgery	Clinical	Continuous
		Treatment progression and care utilisation	PRO	Baseline, annually

Abbreviations: Hip Disability and Osteoarthritis Outcome Score – Physical Function Shortform (HOOS-PS); Health-Related Quality of Life (HRQoL); Knee injury and Osteoarthritis Outcome Score – Physical Function Shortform (KOOS-PS); Numeric Pain Rating Scale (NPR); Patient-Reported Outcome (PRO). Adapted from "Patient-centered outcome measures" by International Consortium for Health Outcomes Measurement, (n.d.). Retrieved November 14, 2022 (https://connect.ichom.org/patient-centered-outcome-measures/). Copyright © by ICHOM Connect.

2.2.3 *Implementation of PROs into Clinical Workflows Connects with Measuring Outcomes*

PROs are a key measurement of the effectiveness of patient-centred care. PRO data could provide complementary information (e.g., clinical exams, laboratory tests and imaging results) in medical decision-making (Snyder et al., 2017). For patients themselves, PROs could provide information on the impact of different treatment options to help them to weigh up the risks and benefits of various treatment options (International Society for Quality of Life Research [ISOQOL], 2015).

PROs should be implemented as a part of clinical workflow. However, PROs are not widely collected and used in clinical practice due to limited time and manpower assessing PROs; limited training on and availability of software for collating patient-reported outcome measures (PROMs); lack of clinically meaningful cut-off points; and a lack of high-quality evidence that PRO assessment improves care (Hsiao et al., 2019; Zhang et al., 2019).

Traditionally, PROs are collected individually using paper-based surveys. The integration of PROs into electronic health records (EHRs) could provide a cost-effective way to collect PROs electronically. However, the main barriers towards ePRO integration have been related to a lack of business case to actionable data, workflow disruption, technical issues and a lack of incentives (Zhang et al., 2019).

Using PROMs will assist in facilitating trends towards patient-centred care and reimbursement for value-health outcomes achieved per dollar spent (Bernstein et al., 2019; van den Hoven et al., 2020; Withers et al., 2021).

2.2.4 *Trends and Issues*

In a recent article, Jansson et al. (2020b) combined PRO and EHR data with clinical quality registries (CQR) to evaluate the effects of a digital tool that supported hip/knee arthroplasty patients through their surgical journey solution. Measures of effectiveness included PROMs, patient-reported experience measures (PREMs), clinical outcomes and costs in using both generic (e.g., EQ-5D-5L) and disease-specific (e.g., WOMAC and OHS/OKS) PROs. In general, CQR collect, analyse and report health information from EHRs and ePROs to enhance quality of care, support clinical decision-making, improve health outcomes, identify best clinical practice and reduce clinical costs (Ruseckaite et al., 2022).

According to findings from Jansson et al. (2020a), data completeness among post-operative PROs was around 85% (unpublished), which is slightly higher than previous literature (Berg et al., 2020), providing an example of how multiple performance metrics might be used simultaneously/effectively in clinical research. In future, multiple data collection modalities (e.g., paper, patient portal and wearables) should be implemented to reduce data collection burden for patients. In addition, machine learning and data science techniques could be applied on PROMs to predict outcomes

Table 2.3 Performance metrics to measure VBHC's quadruple aim

VBHC quadruple aim	*Performance metrics*
Improve patient experience	PREMs; Patient experience survey
Improve health of populations	PROMs; Clinical outcomes Patient-centred outcome measures
Reduce cost of care	Cost outcomes; DRG funding
Improve provider experience	Organisation-related outcomes/experience surveys

(Verma et al., 2021). From an accounting perspective, this study examined the cost-effectiveness of the digital intervention but found that routine hospital data collected for accounting purposes was not able to discriminate between patients, using the digital intervention. Costs borne by the patient and family were outside the funding models but would be included in VBHC analysis. Such costs include transport costs, leave from work borne by patient and families, etc.

The integration of PROMs can improve patient-provider communication (Zhang et al., 2019; Snyder et al., 2019), facilitate shared decision-making, promote self-efficacy, foster patient compliance and enhance patient satisfaction (ISOQOL, 2015). In addition, the integration of PROMs can improve access to healthcare (ISOQOL, 2015), accelerate early detection and enhance management, which can improve efficiency and the quality of life and survival (Brundage et al., 2022). In addition, PROs could be used to support value-based payment models (Leao et al., 2023; Squitieri et al., 2017).

The effective use of validated PROs can play a critical role in improving healthcare delivery and the patient's care experience. Drawing on Iglesia et al. (2020) VBHC's quadruple aim and the associated performance metrics, and the most relevant types of outcome measures, can be divided into PROMs, PREMs, clinical outcomes (health outcomes for the patient), organisation-related outcomes/experience and costs outcomes. This is summarised in Table 2.3.

To date, ICHOM has published 40 sets of patient-centred outcome measures with standardised time points to ensure high-quality research. There is, however, an urgent need to develop and deploy value-based performance metrics from patient, healthcare provider and CQR perspectives (Kennedy et al., 2017) to prioritise a minimum set of outcomes and define feasible, valid and reliable measures to create better value for all stakeholders (International Consortium for Health Outcomes Measurement (n.d.)).

2.2.5 Key Strategies for Successful VBHC Implementation

To ensure improved implementation of VBHC, it is crucial that healthcare professionals receive **VBHC education** via targeted education days or conferences, audit meetings, regular case-based discussions and training. Training is essential when introducing new models, such as traffic light performance measurement systems (using RAG – red, amber and green indicators) risk detection models (Ahluwalia et al., 2019) and new bundled payments (Lichkus et al., 2019). Education of patients is similarly essential. Jansson et al. (2020a) and Lichkus et al. (2019) observed the education requirements of patients using a mobile application for their surgical journey, both within and outside the hospital setting. Providing a user experience pre- and post-discharge comprising educational resources, regular performance measurement log and check-in opportunities to help patients recognise early complications is a strategy to support VBHC implementation.

Another critical aspect to VBHC implementation is **centralised health information technology platforms** to cover the full cycle of care – specifically, this could mean that primary care physicians and specialists use a single or connected IT system (Norton et al., 2019).

Introducing **VBHC pilot projects** in the first phase of implementation is also essential. This is because through pilot projects, longitudinal outcomes and costs per medical condition can eventually be measured, which will allow for the identification of variation in outcomes across the full cycle of care (Dronkers et al., 2020; Nilsson et al., 2017).

Finally ensuring VBHC is implemented with a **multidisciplinary team of experts** comprising employees – clinicians and administrators – from different professional backgrounds (Teisberg et al., 2020).

2.3 VBHC in Australia: An Accounting Perspective

In Australia, a coordinated approach to VBHC is underway and gaining momentum, particularly from around 2018–2019. The VBHC movement is not necessarily under the label 'value-based healthcare' but follows the **quadruple aim** – i.e., improve patient experience, improve population health, reduce cost of care and improve provider experience – which is driving healthcare delivery quality improvements and changes to resource allocation. Insights from adoption process throughout Australia are indicated in the sections that follow.

An inaugural VBHC Conference was convened in Perth in 2021 with Teisberg as plenary speaker to help bring regulators, administrators and clinicians to the debate (https://valuebasedcareaustralia.com.au/events/value-based-health-care-conference/). NSW Health played a leading role in this conference as a recognised leader in the country. The range of initiatives and projects which support the move to VBHC throughout Australia is relatively diverse. For example, the Deeble Institute for Health Policy Research provided initial insights into a VBHC project to support cancer management in Australia. Their project – the Continuous Improvement in Care – Cancer (CIC Cancer Project), aims to create value by improving health outcomes while containing costs (www.ciccancer.com) and is measured by combining clinical information with PROM information (see Figure 2.2).

Although the CIC Cancer Project report is scant on accounting activities to support financial and non-financial performance measurement and resource

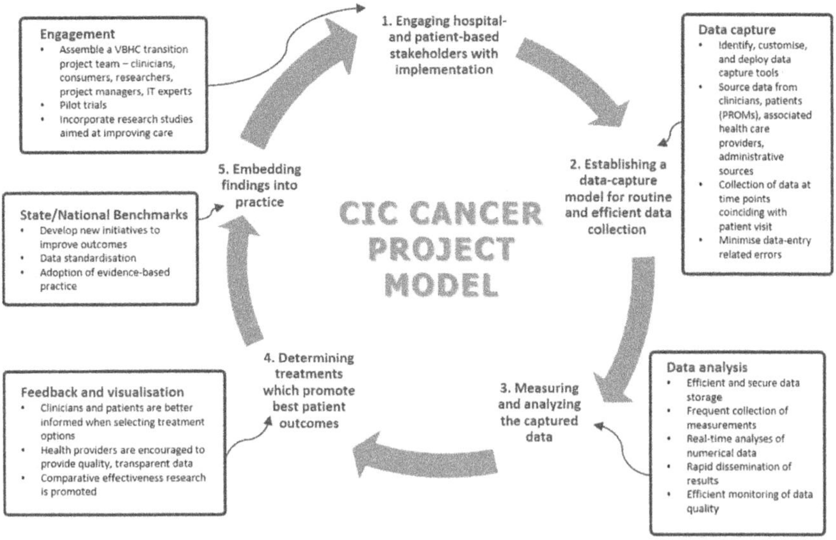

Figure 2.2 CIC Cancer Project Model.

Note: Adapted from "Patients first: The Continuous Improvement in Care -Cancer CIC CANCER PROJECT" by Continuous Improvement in Care Cancer, (n.d.), Retrieved March 14, 2023, from (https://www.ciccancer.com/). Copyright © by Continuous Improvement in Care Cancer. Reprinted with permission.

allocation, the authors do discuss the need for change through technology, along with data analytics and visualisation as part of decision-making support. This book, along with the interviews highlighting the important but lagging role that accounting can play in supporting this emerging approach, fills in some of those gaps.

An example from NSW Health is a **system restructure, designed to highlight key areas** in order to build on the **quadruple aim** and **focus on value-based care delivery**. One of the interviewees explained the changes, commencing with the creation of four value-based programmes – better value care, integrated care, collaborative commissioning and commissioning for better value. The better value care started with eight initiatives where there were large volumes of patients requiring costly medical or surgical interventions. Areas included osteoarthritis (surgical and medical treatment), chronic heart failure, chronic obstructive pulmonary disease, chronic conditions in patients with diabetes, pregnancy and diabetes, high-risk foot falls in hospitals and renal supportive care.

Internationally, these health conditions have well-researched, evidence-based models of care which allow for clear guideline-based performance evaluation. They are also areas in which NSW Health believes it can make a material difference by **wrapping a multidisciplinary team around solutioning.** Currently there are huge variations in care across Australia, with unnecessary waste and hospital readmissions. It is argued that efficiency and effectiveness will follow, as value-based care for patients in these distinct groupings, as identified by NSW Health, are addressed. The system in place in NSW Health, although five years in, is ready for the next stages of change, but there are still challenges and structural issues with managing bundled payments. The interviewee explained that an ideal solution is still being worked through and meanwhile, hospital executives and accountants who do not necessarily understand the funding models, believe that they will lose funding, especially if care is moved from inpatient to outpatient. This adds to a sense of overall reluctance, instead of moving more quickly, as some would like. Added to this, the interviewee argued that **accounting's value analyses are retrospective** with no ability to prospectively use data, in a budgetary sense.

Queensland Health interviews suggested that focusing on VBHC, instead of the quadruple aim, can lead to thinking which is frozen in either costs or disease conditions. Both Queensland Health and NSW Health noted that the VBHC approach, per se, had emerged from the United States and was therefore not in perfect alignment with Australia's healthcare system. While the concept's overall philosophy is guiding change at state government level, both Queensland Health and NSW Health use the **quadruple aim** to manage their digital health strategy, arguing that this approach delivers multiple benefits to the community. Queensland Government Health Horizon takes a staged approach to funding investment, with Horizon 1 providing a single EMR for 70% of all public healthcare in Queensland. It was funded based on long-term benefits, associated with Horizon's three proposed stages. Horizon 1 did not generate any revenue for hospitals but contributed to overall cost savings for total care activities across the health value chain. Horizon 1 aimed to digitise the records. Horizon 2 aimed to extract data and deliver insights back to the business by delivering a learning healthcare system. Horizon 3 focuses on digital workflows and utilising the data to create new models of care. Horizon 1 is future-focussed modelling and would not have met cost-benefit analysis. However, including the vision of Horizons 2 and 3 means Queensland Health can record outcomes and monitor and manage actions in real time. According to Queensland Health, this is the real projected value for the initial investment in VBHC, and where clinicians foresee that AI-generated data will be utilised in clinical decision-making.

In taking an opportunity cost perspective to promote cost-benefit analysis, several interviewees argued that the patient experience can also be measured in cost savings. For example, when patients receive care in their own homes, they do not incur the costs associated with travelling to the hospital. The hospital also incurs a saving by freeing up space for other patient care activities. One interviewee explained that the account's role also becomes one of **co-producer, in this emerging healthcare landscape**. That is, wrapping a multidisciplinary team around problem areas means accounting is recognised as an essential co-producer, in order to help meet the goals of the quadruple aim. A comparative example of the co-producer in healthcare is the 'phlebotomy approach' (i.e., blood sampling) where one blood sample can involve multiple experts – from communicating diagnoses and treatment, to further sampling and co-producing activities for successful health service delivery. This communication channel is also shared internationally to help build a case around standardised care pathways and foster best practice in working towards VBHC.

In a similar way, the Victorian government is striving to ensure the following six key factors are taken into account to ensure early implementation of VBHC is successful:

- Having supportive leadership at all levels, to maintain VBHC as the strategic direction.
- Having clearly defined goals, including why the initiatives are being undertaken.
- Using a robust measurement system that brings together high-quality, reliable data from multiple sources.
- Monitoring and feeding data back to providers, clinicians, patients and other stakeholders.
- Making available educational material and support in using the data – to both clinicians and consumers (i.e., improving data literacy).
- Ensuring accountability for 'actioning' results generated from the monitoring system (Safer Care Victoria, 2019).

Victorian Department of Health interviewees explained how funding has supported new initiatives. In working towards the management of chronic heart disease, one hospital is funded to receive remote ECG data from around the state, where it can be instantly reviewed to determine the need for hospitalisation. This saves on unnecessary admissions. Further, the introduction of Australia's first heart hospital (https://victorianhearthospital.org/) offers the opportunity to introduce VBHC strategies in a research-intensive site. Evidence provided from extant studies, such as a US bundled-payment programme for heart failure (Lichkus et al., 2019), will support accountants and possibly provide a pilot site for the development of an Australian model based on VBHC principles. Further investigation of the accounting activities in this new setting is required.

The COVID-19 pandemic also saw an expansion of Hospital in the Home (HITH) programmes. HITH provides value-based care by transferring patients from hospital to receive ongoing care in their own homes. HITH frees up hospital beds, while ensuring that patients continue to receive necessary treatments such as wound dressings, chemotherapy, intravenous antibiotics and more. Again, the accounting is lagging with debates over how this is funded and the general practitioner's (GP) voice is somewhat absent in the hospital-delivered home-based care. More research is required to see how these new approaches are undertaken from a funding perspective. Funding models and approaches to bundled care will be covered in more detail in the following chapter.

Box 2.1 Insights from Finland

Given the opportunity to obtain evidence from Finland, through project collaboration as well as an interview with a leading VBHC expert in Helsinki, we can provide insights into what has been achieved in Finland to date, as well as that country's future direction. As an adviser to Finland's Ministry for Social and Health Affairs and the Ministry of Finance, the expert insights provide the opportunity for a deeper understanding of VBHC in Finland, as well as providing a basis for Australian comparative analysis.

Currently Finland is restructuring its social and healthcare system and associated funding. They are now allocating funds to local districts mostly based on healthcare needs (e.g., current demand for services). In this way, funding is provided for the management of *all* social and healthcare needs within that district, giving senior leaders the opportunity to manage both investment and operational costs for all associated care expenditure, from primary healthcare to tertiary hospital service delivery. While budgeting based on needs appears to be an antithesis to VBHC, this is a designated starting point with the main aim of this **structural reform** to drive better performance management.

Performance measurement of outcomes is currently underway and is being measured directly and indirectly, through a separate measurement scheme. In Finland, a primary care patient grouping system (pDRG) segments patients into groups (e.g., diabetes, cardiovascular, musculoskeletal disease, cancer, etc.). The pDRG has been developed for measuring complete care episodes. However, it is still not yet officially used. The expert claims it still is in the process of being developed, because some patients may have co-morbidities (i.e., more than one disease condition at a time) which makes it hard to determine which is the major condition to dominate outcome measurement. Also, the measurement time periods need to be contained for comparability. In some chronic conditions, annual cost follow-ups may be required. Measurement includes direct cost of treatment as well as indirect measures, i.e., ability for a patient to return to work, sick leave, early retirement and use of resources. The outcome measurement will be based on 'national quality registers' which started about five years ago, in areas such as diabetes, heart disease, back pain, psychosis, etc. In addition, some diseases like cancer and arthritis have had national quality registers already earlier. To date the National Institute for Health and Welfare in Finland has National Quality Registers for nine patient groups covering around 50% of the disease burden (DALY) which forms the basis of their approach to outcome measurement. The quality registers focus on measuring clinical and PROs and Finnish national registers enable collection of most relevant patient-level direct and indirect costs and linking them on an individual level.

For example, if a patient has a hip fracture or breast cancer, their individual costs can be tracked throughout their treatment journey. This would include general practitioner, pharmacy, radiology and allied health costs, as well as inpatient hospital costs associated with their surgical intervention. In addition, the indirect costs such as sick leave costs can be measured as well from the registries. Measurement continues until the patient returns to a pre-defined position. From a medical perspective, successful outcomes from hip surgery would be 90 days at home without any assistance. For cancer treatment, it would be one year disease-free. But as this does not truly measure quality of life (i.e., how patients are managing their home and working lives, with/without family support, etc.), Finland is also looking at simple measures to further enhance outcomes measurement. The expert argued that 'scientific' ways of measuring outcomes capturing all potentially relevant dimensions could potentially overload patients and may not be possible. Instead, Finland is seeking to identify a minimal viable set for measuring and start with that.

One crucial factor that makes data collection and measurement easier in Finland is that all residents have a unique ID from birth, which travels with them across the lifespan, providing a longitudinal record of all social and health-related resourcing utilised by the individual, across the country.

More detail of how funds are allocated will be provided in Chapter 3.

In summary, it is argued that to manage a value-based approach in Australia, governments must foster the opportunity to scale successful pilots, such as the CIC Cancer Project, at not only a local but international scale. As identified in the current activities in Finland, government must develop data standards on how to measure value and have the capabilities to track, digest and act on outcomes while providing aligned cost data to support resource allocation. It is proposed that evidence, generated by independent academics, is needed to inform decisions by policymakers, payers, providers and investors (Maru et al., 2019, p. 7).

2.4 Implications for Accounting

Our findings indicate that Australia is further behind in the VBHC journey than other parts of the world. In comparison with the most advanced countries (e.g., France, Italy and San Marino (Cooper, 2022)), there is still further work required in Australia to educate, integrate information systems and establish pilot-based performance evaluation using financial and non-financial metrics. Drawing on these findings, we have further adapted Table 1.1 to show how accountants can be supportive in the implementation of VBHC strategies, while considering the competing values of multiple stakeholders. Each is depicted in Table 2.4.

Table 2.4 A strategic values-based framework for VBHC implementation: Accounting impacts

Strategy/Values	*How can accountants support?*
Understand the shared health needs of patients Measure health outcomes and costs	Detail current VBHC activities, **reconfigured structures** and provide insights into value-based non-financial **performance measurements** that understand the immediate health needs of patients. **Assist:** Engagement with non-financial performance metrics that matter to patients.
Industrial value	The system is still managing the conflict between siloed structures and the emergence of new VBHC-inspired structures around costly patient groupings. **Assist:** Ensure accounting budget solutions can support the new VBHC structures.
Market value	There is growing market demand for VBHC. Clinicians are leading as it makes more sense to measure ROI in terms of patient outcomes. However, the cost component of the equation is not meeting short-term ROI but being measured longitudinally with arguments for a staged approach to maximise final goals. **Assist:** Improved measurement to avoid dysfunctional decisions with short-term ROI.
Domestic value	There is a conflict over traditional approaches and the VBHC change movement. Hierarchy is taking the lead with accounting seen as the blocker to change. **Assist:** VBHC education and training around solutioning; accounting to be a co-producer.
Civic value	Health departments are taking the lead, but with jurisdictional differences. Quadruple aim appears to be the guiding principle for regulatory oversight. **Assist:** VBHC performance metrics that are simple, manageable and goal-oriented.
Inspired value	Solutioning so far is clinically inspired; accounting inspired value is stagnant. **Assist:** Provide improved support for accounting to move from a retrospective to a prospective co-producer.
Fame value	The VBHC movement is using international influencers and generating their own. Influencers are largely from government, clinical and health economics backgrounds. **Assist:** Accounting to create their own influencers to ensure they are key to change.

2.5 Conclusion

In essence, this chapter contributes to the VBHC discourse by manifolds. It contributes by providing a comprehensive exploration of its multifaceted nature of VBHC model, its implications for stakeholders and the actionable steps required to successfully embed it into healthcare systems.

1 **Definition of VBHC:** The chapter provides a comprehensive introduction to VBHC, by considering key definitions of VBHC, elucidating its potential impact on healthcare systems and the broader understanding of 'value' within healthcare delivery processes.
2 **Value's Multifaceted Definition:** Building upon the work of experts like Gray (2015), this chapter expands the traditional understanding of 'value'. It does so by delineating it into allocative, technical, personalised and societal categories, moving beyond a mere focus on costs and cost-effectiveness viewpoint.
3 **Patient-Centricity:** Emphasising the heterogeneity of patient perspectives, as highlighted by Duckett (2019), the chapter underscores the complexity of translating VBHC rhetoric into actionable policies and practices.
4 **Healthcare System Transition:** This chapter's contribution is that it maps the ongoing transition from volume-driven to value-driven care models. It provides detailed discussion on the benefits of this transition, such as reduced costs for both healthcare providers and patients, increased focus on preventive healthcare services and better overall patient outcomes.
5 **Significance of PROs:** This chapter's contribution stems from highlighting the crucial role of PROs; the chapter explores their potential in refining patient-centred care. It also discusses the barriers to their broader adoption and the potential benefits of integrating PROs into digital or electronic health record systems.
6 **Australian VBHC Landscape:** Offering insights into Australia's healthcare scene, the chapter traces the country's VBHC journey, emphasising pivotal initiatives like the Continuous Improvement in Care – Cancer Project. It also highlights the country's position compared to global leaders (like Finland) in VBHC.
7 **Accounting's Role in VBHC:** One of the central contributions of this chapter is its exploration of the gap between VBHC principles and accounting practices. It offers actionable takeaways for accountants, suggesting how they can become integral players in the VBHC transformation.
8 **Key Takeaways for VBHC Implementation:** The chapter culminates with five principal takeaways, providing a roadmap for stakeholders. These include understanding patient perspectives, embracing stakeholder collaboration, emphasising the importance of education in VBHC, integrating data and emerging technologies into clinical workflows and advocating for a unified VBHC strategy across regions.

In conclusion, the discussion in this chapter has provided five key takeaways for accountants to proactively support value-based performance evaluation and change.

Key Takeaway 1: Understanding what matters to patients themselves is fundamental to improving healthcare. Accountants can support in the standardisation of outcome measures that matter to patients for improved management and evidence for value-based payment.

Key Takeaway 2: Multiple stakeholder perspectives need to be considered when developing and deploying value metrics for individual patient care pathways and scaling VBHC pilots in areas of chronic disease management. Accounting should play an important co-producer role, particularly in budgeting for new VBHC structures.

Key Takeaway 3: Education is required to ensure long-term budgeting and investment for VBHC change, and addressing this conflict can improve the provider experience.

Key Takeaway 4: There is a need to develop data analysis and visualisation tools to integrate data into clinical workflows to guide clinical decision-making. In addition, emerging AI machine-learning techniques require accountants to embrace PROMs to predict outcomes and associated costs.

Key Takeaway 5: VBHC implementation requires resourcing strategy and uniformity across Australia. All technical, logistical, social and organisational barriers (e.g., workflow configuration, incentives and state/territory-based initiatives) need to be solved for improved alignment. Addressing this conflict would help enhance the provider experience.

References

Ahluwalia, R., Cook, J., Raheman, F., Karuppaiah, K., Colegate-Stone, T., Tavakkolizadeh, A., Kavarthapu, V., & Sinha, J. (2021). Improving the efficiency of ankle fracture care through home care and day-surgery units: Delivering safe surgery on a value-based healthcare model. *The Surgeon*, *19*(5), e95–e102. 10.1016/j.surge.2020.08.004

Ahluwalia, R., Vainieri, E., Tam, J., Sait, S., Sinha, A., Manu, C. A., Reichert, I., Kavarthapu, V., Edmonds, M., & Vas, P. (2019). Surgical diabetic foot debridement: Improving training and practice utilizing the traffic light principle. *The International Journal of Lower Extremity Wounds*, *18*(3), 279–286. 10.1177/1534734619853657

Andersson, A. E., Baathe, F., Wikstrom, E., & Nilsson, K. (2015). Understanding value-based healthcare – An interview study with project team members at a Swedish university hospital. *Journal of Hospital Administration*, *4*(4), 64–72. 10.5430/jha.v4n4p64

Berg, U., W-Dahl, A., Rolfson, O., Nauclér, E., Sundberg, M., & Nilsdotter, A. (2020). Influence of fast-track programs on patient-reported outcomes in total hip and knee replacement (THR/TKR) at Swedish hospitals 2011–2015: An observational study including 51,169 THR and 8,393 TKR operations. *Acta Orthopaedica*, *91*(3), 306–312. 10.1080/17453674.2020.1733375

Bernstein, A., Gustafson, M. T., & Lewis, R. (2019). Disaster on the horizon: The price effect of sea level rise. *Journal of Financial Economics*, *134*(2), 253–272. 10.1016/j.jfineco.2019.03.013

Brundage, M. D., Crossnohere, N. L., O'Donnell, J., Cruz Rivera, S., Wilson, R., Wu, A. W., Moher, D., Kyte, D., Reeve, B. B., Gilbert, A., Chen, R. C., Calvert, M. J., & Snyder, C. (2022). Listening to the patient voice adds value to cancer clinical trials. *Journal of the National Cancer Institute*, *114*(10), 1323–1332. 10.1093/jnci/djac128.

Continuous Improvement in Care Cancer. (n.d.). *Patients First: The Continuous Improvement in Care -Cancer CIC CANCER PROJECT*. Retrieved March 14, 2023, from https://www.ciccancer.com/

Cooper, W. (2022, December 28). Which countries have the best healthcare in the world. *William Russell*. Retrieved April 12, 2023, from https://www.william-russell.com/blog/countries-worlds-best-healthcare-systems/

Douglas, C., Aroh, D., Colella, J., & Quadri, M. (2016). The HackensackUMC value-based care model. *Nursing Administration Quarterly*, *40*(1), 51–59. 10.1097/NAQ.0000000000000136

Dronkers, E. A., Baatenburg de Jong, R. J., van Der Poel, E. F., Sewnaik, A., & Offerman, M. P. (2020). Keys to successful implementation of routine symptom monitoring in head and neck oncology with "Healthcare Monitor" and patients' perspectives of quality of care. *Head & Neck*, *42*(12), 3590–3600. 10.1002/hed.26425

Duckett, S. (2019). Value-based health care–fad or fabulous? *Healthcare Papers*, *18*(3), 15–21.

Duckett, S., Daniels, S., Kamp, M., Stockwell, A., Walker, G., & Ward, M. (2008). Pay for performance in Australia: Queensland's new clinical practice improvement payment. *Journal of Health Services Research & Policy*, *13*(3), 174–177. 10.1258/jhsrp.2008.007178

Featherall, J., Brigati, D. P., Arney, A. N., Faour, M., Bokar, D. V., Murray, T. G., Molloy, R. M., & Higuera Rueda, C. A. (2019). Effects of a Total knee arthroplasty care pathway on cost, quality, and patient experience: Toward measuring the triple aim. *The Journal of Arthroplasty*, *34*(11), 2561–2568. 10.1016/j.arth.2019.06.011

Goretti, G., Marinari, G. M., Vanni, E., & Ferrari, C. (2020). Value-based healthcare and enhanced recovery after surgery implementation in a high-volume bariatric center in Italy. *Obesity Surgery*, *30*, 2519–2527. 10.1007/s11695-020-04464-w

Gray, M. (2015). The 'triple value agenda' must be our focus this century. *NHS Confederation*. https://www.nhsconfed.org/articles/triple-value-agenda-must-be-our-focus-century

Hsiao, C. J., Dymek, C., Kim, B., & Russell, B. (2019). Advancing the use of patient-reported outcomes in practice: Understanding challenges, opportunities, and the potential of health information technology. *Quality of Life Research*, *28*(6), 1575–1583. 10.1007/s11136-019-02112-0

Iglesia, E. G. A., Greenhawt, M., & Shaker, M. S. (2020). Achieving the quadruple aim to deliver value-based allergy care in an ever-evolving healthcare system. *Annals of Allergy, Asthma & Immunology*, *125*(2), 126–366. 10.1016/j.anai.2020.04.007

International Consortium for Health Outcomes Measurement. (n.d.). *Patient-Centered Outcome Measures*. Retrieved November 14, 2022, from https://connect.ichom.org/patient-centered-outcome-measures/

International Society for Quality of Life Research. (2015). *User's guide to implementing patient-reported outcomes assessment in clinical practice*. International Society for Quality of Life Research. https://www.isoqol.org/wp-content/uploads/2019/09/2015UsersGuide-Version2.pdf

Jansson, M. M., Hyvämäki, P., & Pikkarainen, M. (2020a). Computer- and telephone-delivered interventions on patient outcome and resource utilization in patients with orthopedic conditions: A systematic review and narrative synthesis. *Orthopaedic Nursing*, *39*(5), 340–352. 10.1097/NOR.0000000000000699

Jansson, M. M., Vuorinen, A. L., Harjumaa, M., Pikkarainen, M., Similä, H., Koivisto, J., Puhto, A. P., & Vesty, G. (2020b). The digital patient journey solution for patients undergoing elective hip and knee arthoplasty due to primary osteoarthritis: Protocol for a pragmatic randomized controlled trial. *Journal of Advanced Nursing*, *76*(6), 1436–1448. 10.1111/jan.14343

Kaplan, R. S. (2020). Using the balanced scorecard for successful health care M&A integration. *NEJM Catalyst Innovations in Care Delivery*, *1*(3). https://catalyst.nejm.org/doi/full/10.1056/CAT.20.0286

Kennedy, B. M., Rehman, M., Johnson, W. D., Magee, M. B., Leonard, R., & Katzmarzyk, P. T. (2017). Healthcare providers versus patients' understanding of health beliefs and values. *Patient Experience Journal*, *4*(3), 29–37. https://www.ncbi.nlm.nih.gov/pmc/articles/PMC5751953/

Kurt, P., Saban, M., Cankaya, F., & Annac, M. C. (2019). Time-driven activity-based costing in the ophthalmology department of state hospital: a case study. *Fresenius Environmental Bulletin*, *28*(4), 2754–2770.

Leao, D. L. L., Cremers, H. P., van Veghel, D., Pavlova, M., Hafkamp, F. J., & Groot, W. N. J. (2023). Facilitating and inhibiting factors in the design, implementation, and applicability of value-based payment models: A systematic literature review. *Medical Care Research and Review*, 10.1177/10775587231160920

Lichkus, J., Wolf, C., Hynds, R., Moorer, K., Bourgoine, D., Garabedian, N., & Eamranond, P. (2019). Effect of implementing a bundled-payment program for heart failure at a safety-net community hospital. *Population Health Management*, *22*(1), 12–18. 10.1089/pop.2018.0001

Lundström, M., & Pesudovs, K. (2009). Catquest-9SF patient outcomes questionnaire: Nine-item short-form Rasch-scaled revision of the Catquest questionnaire. *Journal of Cataract & Refractive Surgery*, 35(3), 504–513. 10.1016/j.jcrs.2008.11.038

Maru, C., Lin, A., Kagubare, K., Pollack, A., Stern, A., Rao, N., & Walker, J. (2019). *Leapfrog to Value: How nations can adopt value-based care on the path to universal health coverage*. Leapfrog to Value. https://static1.squarespace.com/static/5db772d44638535b2114f2e6/t/5ddea52751c72e2c5edacd77/1574872363413/2019_LeapfrogToValue.pdf

Miao, Y., Yuan, X., Gu, J., Zhang, L., He, R., Sandeep, S., & Wu, J. (2019). Constructing a value-based healthcare system for hypertensive patients through changing payment mode: Evidence from a comparative study in rural China. *Journal of Medical Economics*, *22*(3), 245–251. 10.1080/13696998.2018.1558864

Miller, H. D. (2009). From volume to value: Better ways to pay for health care. *Health Affairs (Project Hope)*, *28*(5), 1418–1428. 10.1377/hlthaff.28.5.1418

Mkanta, W. N., Katta, M., Basireddy, K., English, G., & de Grubb, M. C. M. (2016). Theoretical and methodological issues in research related to value-based approaches in healthcare. *Journal of Healthcare Management*, *61*(6), 402–419.

Montesinos Gálvez, A. C., Jódar Sánchez, F., Alcántara Moreno, C., Pérez Fernández, A. J., Benítez García, R., Coca López, M., Bienvenido Ramírez, M. P., Cabrera López, M., Vázquez Burrero, L., Jurado Berja, P., Sánchez García, R., Cebrián, J. M., Hervas García, M. L., López Fernández, R., Pérez Jiménez, C., Reyes Vico, M. A., Vargas Villegas, A. B., García-Agua Soler, N., & García Ruiz, A. J. (2020). Value-based healthcare in ostomies. *International Journal of Environmental Research and Public Health*, *17*(16), 5879. 10.3390/ijerph17165879

NEJM Catalyst. (2017). What is value-based healthcare. *Massachusetts Medical Society*. https://catalyst.nejm.org/doi/full/10.1056/CAT.17.0558

Nilsson, K., Bååthe, F., Andersson, A. E., Wikström, E., & Sandoff, M. (2017). Experiences from implementing value-based healthcare at a Swedish University Hospital–a longitudinal interview study. *BMC Health Services Research*, *17*(1), 1–12. 10.1186/s12913-017-2104-8

Norton, P. T., Rodriguez, H. P., Shortell, S. M., & Lewis, V. A. (2019). Organizational influences on health care system adoption and use of advanced health information technology capabilities. *The American Journal of Managed Care*, *25*(1), e21. https://www.ncbi.nlm.nih.gov/pmc/articles/PMC6581444/

Porter, M. E., & Teisberg, E. O. (2006). *Redefining health care: Creating value-based competition on results*. Harvard Business Press.

Porter, M. E. (2009). A strategy for health care reform – Toward a value-based system. *The New England Journal of Medicine*, *361*(2), 109–112. 10.1056/NEJMp0904131

Putera, I. (2017). Redefining health: Implication for value-based healthcare reform. *Cureus*, *9*(3), e1067. 10.7759/cureus.1067

Ruseckaite, R., Maharaj, A. D., Dean, J., Krysinska, K., Ackerman, I. N., Brennan, A. L., Busija, L., Carter, H., Earnest, A., Forrest, C. B., Harris, I. A., Sansoni, J., & Ahern, S. (2022). Preliminary development of recommendations for the inclusion of patient-reported outcome measures in clinical quality registries. *BMC Health Services Research*, *22*(1), 276. 10.1186/s12913-022-07657-4

Safer Care Victoria. (2019). Local and international perspectives on value based health care. Retrieved from https://www.safercare.vic.gov.au/news-and-media/local-and-international-perspectives-on-value-based-health-care

Snyder, C., & Wu, A. W. (2017). *Users' guide to integrating patient-reported outcomes in electronic health records*. John Hopkins University. https://www.pcori.org/sites/default/files/PCORI-JHU-Users-Guide-To-Integrating-Patient-Reported-Outcomes-in-Electronic-Health-Records.pdf

Snyder, C., Brundage, M., Rivera, Y. M., & Wu, A. W. (2019). A PRO-cision medicine methods toolkit to address the challenges of personalizing cancer care using patient-reported outcomes: Introduction to the supplement. *Medical Care*, *57*, S1–S7. 10.1097/MLR.0000000000001089

Squitieri, L., Bozic, K. J., & Pusic, A. L. (2017). The role of patient-reported outcome measures in value-based payment reform. *Value Health*, *20*(6), 834–836. 10.1016/j.jval.2017.02.003

Teisberg, E., Wallace, S., & O'Hara, S. (2020). Defining and implementing value-based health care: a strategic framework. *Academic Medicine*, *95*(5), 682. 10.1097/ACM.0000000000003122

van den Hoven, A. T., Bons, L. R., Dykgraaf, R. H. M., Dessens, A. B., Pastoor, H., de Graaff, L. C. G., Metselaar, M. R., Kneppers-Swets, A., Kardys, I., Mijnarends, H., Zweerus, F., Hazelzet, J. A., Utens, E. M. W. J., van den Bosch, A. E., & Roos-Hesselink, J. W. (2020). A value-based healthcare approach: Health-related quality of life and psychosocial functioning in women with Turner syndrome. *Clinical Endocrinology (Oxford)*, *92*(5), 434–442. 10.1111/cen.14166

van Veghel, D., Daeter, E. J., Bax, M., Amoroso, G., Blaauw, Y., Camaro, C., Cummins, P., Halfwerk, F. R., Wijdh-den Hamer, I. J., de Jong, J. S. S. G., Stooker, W., van der Wees, P. J., & van der Nat, P. B. (2020a). Organization of outcome-based quality improvement in Dutch heart centres. *European Heart Journal. Quality of Care & Clinical Outcomes*, *6*(1), 49–54. 10.1093/ehjqcco/qcz021 van Veghel, D., Soliman-Hamad, M., Schulz, D. N., Cost, B., Simmers, T. A., & Dekker, L. R. (2020b). Improving clinical outcomes and patient satisfaction among patients with coronary artery disease: An example of enhancing regional integration between a cardiac centre and a referring hospital. *BMC Health Services Research*, *20*, 1–8.

Verma, D., Bach, K., & Mork, P. J. (2021). Application of machine learning methods on patient reported outcome measurements for predicting outcomes: A literature review. *Informatics*, *8*(3), 56. 10.3390/informatics8030056

WHO (2020). Global strategy on digital health 2020–2025. Available at: https://www.who.int/publications-detail-redirect/9789240020924

Withers, K., Palmer, R., Lewis, S., & Carolan-Rees, G. (2021). First steps in PROMs and PREMs collection in Wales as part of the prudent and value-based healthcare agenda. *Quality of Life Research*, *30*, 3157–3170. 10.1007/s11136-020-02711-2

Zeithaml, V. A., Parasuraman, A., & Berry, L. L. (1990). *Delivering quality service: Balancing customer perceptions and expectations*. Free Press.

Zhang, R., Burgess, E. R., Reddy, M. C., Rothrock, N. E., Bhatt, S., Rasmussen, L. V., Butt, Z., & Starren, J. B. (2019). Provider perspectives on the integration of patient-reported outcomes in an electronic health record. *JAMIA Open*, *2*(1), 73–80. 10.1093/jamiaopen/ooz001

3 Activity-Based Funding Models and Investment Appraisal

Gillian Vesty, Miia Jansson, Tarek Rana, Kerryn Butler-Henderson, and Vijayajothy Jayakumar

3.1 Introduction

Australia's approach to implementing value-based healthcare (VBHC) is largely through the **quadruple aim** – i.e., *improve patient experience, improve population health, reduce cost of care and improve provider experience.* Chapter 2 highlighted this approach and largely focused on understanding the patient experience and population health through improved performance evaluation. However, it is argued that for effective implementation of VBHC, attention also needs to be given to **designing payment models** that reward the highest value of care. To date, empirical evidence confirms that the introduction of bundled payments results in reduced cost of care, decreased admission to skilled nursing facilities and lowered readmission rates (Lichkus et al., 2019; Miao et al., 2019). Chapter 2 revealed certain conflicts around the management of the cost of care and the lack of bundled payments in Australia which is resulting in conflicts while negating provider experience. To address this issue, this chapter will focus on the links between performance evaluation and healthcare payments by governments. The aim is to provide a greater understanding of the models for the management of budgets from an operational and strategic investment perspective.

3.2 Hospital Funding Models

> Neither the volume- and profit-based approach pursued by private providers, nor the access-first strategy embraced by the public sector responds to the health needs of patients nor maximizes population health. This is a huge waste of public and family funds. The alternative proposed is value-based care, defined here as using outcome and cost data to direct providers to improve delivery through **performance-linked payment.**
>
> (Maru et al., 2019, p. 3)

In this chapter, the focus will be on the **pay** aspect of Maru et al.'s (2019) **measure, deliver** and **pay** model detailed in their flagship report. To understand the process of moving to accounting for VBHC, it is important

DOI: 10.4324/9781032685489-3

to understand the current position in terms of healthcare funding and resource allocation methods. In Australia, the healthcare budget represents 10.6% of GDP and comprises funds for public hospitals, private hospitals, medical and dental services, community health and other practitioners, public health, pharmaceuticals and other medications, patient transport, aids and appliances, administration and capital expenditure. The funding of healthcare is not from a single source but made up of federal and state funding, individuals, health insurers as well as other non-government sources. The Council of Australian Governments oversees the National Health Reform Agreement, which outlines the shared intention of the Commonwealth and state and territory governments. The agreement factors in overall growth in Commonwealth funding. However, this is capped at 6.5% a year (the National Funding Cap). The aim is that both state and national governments work in partnership to improve health outcomes for all Australians and ensure the sustainability of the Australian health system.

The different health funding flows in Australia are outlined in Table 3.1. This is followed by Table 3.2 which highlights the different input funds, discussed in more detail in the following sections.

Of significant interest is the research and capital expenditure which is largely managed by grants. As such, government healthcare service providers in Australia are treated as cost centres with costs reimbursed, while investment relies on grant activity. Two main types of payments for public hospitals are distributed from the pool of **activity-based funding** (ABF) and **block funding**.

Block funding is a mode of funding, recognised as the traditional funding model whereby the government provides grants to approved providers to deliver services. In general, categories of block funding include teaching, training and research, small rural hospitals, non-admitted mental health, non-admitted Child and Adolescent Mental Health Services (CAMHS), non-admitted home ventilation, other non-admitted services (e.g., chronic disease management) and highly specialised therapies (see https://www.publichospitalfunding.gov.au/public-hospital-funding/funding-types). ABF is discussed in more detail in the following subsection.

3.2.1 *Activity-Based Funding*

ABF is the government funding method for public hospital services. ABF is based on the number of weighted services provided to patients, that is volume output of hospitals.

The price to be paid for delivering those services is based on a national classifications system. The system is built around **diagnosis-related group** (DRG) codes for the different patient treatment or service types. In total there are 794 different DRG classifications. Understandably, some of the medical/surgical treatments are more expensive than others, and some patients will stay in hospital longer than others, measured as **average length of stay** (ALOS)

Table 3.1 Detailed health spending flows 2019–2020 in Australia

Area of expenditure		*Source of funds*				
		Government		*Non-government*		
		Australian government $86,418m (42.67%)	*State and local government $56,201m (27.75%)*	*Individuals $29,777m (14.7%)*	*Health insurance funds $16,666m (8.23%)*	*Other non-government $13,484m (6.66%)*
Hospitals $83,457m (41.20%)	Public hospital $66,384m (32.77%)	$26,841	$34,868	$1,280	$944	$2,451
	Private hospital $17,073m (8.43%)	$4,543	$1,053	$1,511	$8,561	$1,405
Primary Healthcare $66,949m (33.05)	Unreferred medical services $13,349m (6.59%)	$11,254	–	$820	–	$1,275
	Dental services $9,548m (4.71%)	$1,224	$857	$5,510	$1,909	$48
	Other health practitioners $5,652m (2.79%)	$2,522	$8	$1,617	$840	$665
	Community health and other $10,971m (4.97%)	$1,421	$8,260	$74	–	$315
	Public health $3,591m (1.77%)	$1,932	$1,503	$17	–	$139
	Benefit-paid pharmaceuticals $12,864m (6.35%)	$11,354	–	$1,510	–	–

(Continued)

Table 3.1 (Continued)

Area of expenditure		*Source of funds*				
		Government		*Non-government*		
		Australian government $86,418m (42.67%)	*State and local government $56,201m (27.75%)*	*Individuals $29,777m (14.7%)*	*Health insurance funds $16,666m (8.23%)*	*Other non-government $13,484m (6.66%)*
	All other medications $11,873m (5.86%)	$774	–	$10,957	$45	$97
Referred medical services $20,245m (10.00%)		15,294	$15,294	–	$3,259	$1,693
Other services $14,085m (6.95%)	Patient transport services $4,552m (2.25%)	$354	$3,262	$503	$292	$141
	Aids and appliances $4,412m (2.18%)	$874	–	$2,705	$702	$131
	Administration $5,121m (2.53%)	$2,628	$799	$11	$1,680	$3
Research $6,665 million (3.29%)		5,288	$5,288	$947	$3	–
Capital expenditure $11,145 million (5.50%)		115	$115	$4,643	–	–

Note
Adapted from "Digital health" by the Australian Institute of Health and Welfare database on healthcare expenditure, 2022 (https://www.aihw.gov.au/reports/australias-health/digital-health). Copyright © 2022 by the Australian Institute of Health and Welfare.

Table 3.2 The structure and funding of Australia's health system

Area of expenditure	*Source of funds*				
	Government		*Non-government*		
	Australian government	*State and local government*	*Individuals*	*Private health insurance providers*	*Other non-government*
Hospitals	⇨ ABF ⇨ Block funding ⇨ NPPs ⇨ PHI	⇨ ABF ⇨ Block funding ⇨ Other Programs	⇨ Fees for service	⇨ Benefit payments	⇨ Payments for goods and services
Primary healthcare	⇨ MBS ⇨ PBS ⇨ Dental ⇨ Other programs	⇨ MBS ⇨ PBS ⇨ Other programs	⇨ Fees for service	⇨ Benefit payments	⇨ Payments for goods and services
Referred medical services	⇨ MBS ⇨ Other programs	–	⇨ Fees for service	⇨ Benefit payments	–
Other services	⇨ Direct payments ⇨ Program payments	⇨ Direct payments	⇨ Fees for service	⇨ Benefit payments	⇨ Payments for goods and services
Research	⇨ Grants	⇨ Grants	⇨ Donations	–	⇨ Grants
Capital	⇨ Grants	⇨ Grants	–	–	⇨ Grants

Note
Adapted from "Digital health" by the Australian Institute of Health and Welfare database on healthcare expenditure, 2022 (https://www.aihw.gov.au/reports/australias-health/digital-health). Copyright © 2022 by the Australian Institute of Health and Welfare.

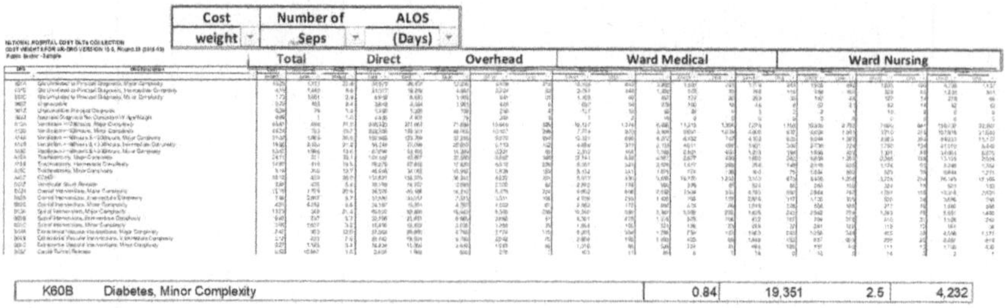

Figure 3.1 National Hospital Cost Data.

Note: Adapted from "NWAU calculators" by the Independent Health and Aged Care Pricing Authority, 2022 (https://www.ihacpa.gov.au/health-care/pricing/nwau-calculators). Copyright © 2022 by the Independent Health and Aged Care Pricing Authority.

which depends on the medical care provided. Treatments are weighted according to their acuity and allocated a **national weighted activity unit** (NWAU). This is a standard cost weight determined by the activity-based costs incurred by an average patient allocated to the DRG. An example of the DRG coding system and national hospital cost data is provided in Figure 3.1.

In this illustration, the DRG code, K60B (indicated in the bottom box) is allocated to a patient admitted to hospital with diabetes (minor level of complexity). The NWAU weighting determined for this code is 0.84. In a year, there were 19,351 patients with minor complexity diabetes in public hospitals (Number of Separations (Seps) = 19,351) and an ALOS of 2.5 days for this patient type. These standards form the basis of payment with the total cost or payment made by government to the hospital being $4,232. The payment price for a weighting of 1.0 is approximately $5,000 and is independently determined by the Independent Health and Aged Care Pricing Authority (IHACPA). This figure ($5,000) is referred to as the National Efficient Price. The term 'activity-based' is given, as each of the activities (ward nursing, ward medical, intensive care, pharmacy, radiology, cleaning, administration, etc.) are calculated for each of the DRGs. The total direct and indirect cost is a culmination of these activity costs.

In Figure 3.2 an overview of the coding information is provided along with the detailed formula of how the payment is costed with a given admission DRG. This formula now includes COVID-19 complications. Payment is determined based on state/territory, hospital, patient demographics, admission diagnosis and whether any risk factors are involved such as falls, surgical or medical complications. These are labelled as **hospital-acquired complication** (HAC) flags.

As indicated in the tables, a significant proportion of healthcare funding is in the form of ABF with annual conditions imposed by the funding bodies to allow for growth, rewards and penalties for underperformance. The following service categories tend to be ABF-funded: emergency department

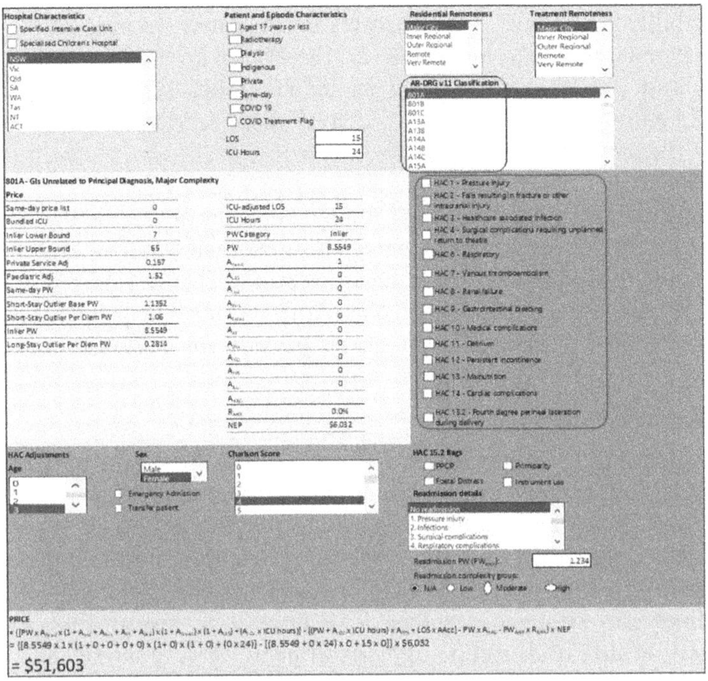

Source: Adapted from https://www.ihacpa.gov.au/health-care/pricing/nwau-calculators

Figure 3.2 NWAU23 Calculator for Acute Activity Payment.

Note: Adapted from "NWAU calculators" by the Independent Health and Aged Care Pricing Authority, 2022 (https://www.ihacpa.gov.au/health-care/pricing/nwau-calculators). Copyright © 2022 by the Independent Health and Aged Care Pricing Authority.

services, acute admitted services, admitted mental health services, sub-acute and non-acute services and some non-admitted services. Hospital in the Home (HITH) is classified as a hospital admission.

Although volume-based payments, ABF arguably provides a powerful incentive for hospitals to perform as efficiently as possible, maximising services provided for the available funds. The proposed advantages of taking an ABF approach are as follows:

- It is **person-centred**, in that the funding is tied to the treatment of people, not simply the funding of an organisation or the size and characteristics of a population.
- It is **information rich** – generating useful data on what services are provided to whom and at what cost across many different types of hospitals and services, enabling better understanding of the provision of hospital services.
- It is **transparent**, making clear on what basis funding is provided, with less opportunity for funding based upon influence or special pleading.

- It also **increases hospital autonomy** to deliver care within a clear funding and accountability framework – it separates and clarifies the role of the funder to determine, and be accountable for, the overall level of services to be provided and the level of funding to deliver those services, while requiring (and empowering) hospitals to deliver those services in the best possible way (Bennett, 2009).

Another long-term benefit of the national implementation of ABF is that it creates stronger incentives for governments to examine their relative level of investment in public hospitals and other health services. Further, ABF is an important tool in allocative efficiency, or seeking to ensure that payment is made for the 'right' health services at the 'right' price in the 'right' setting.

3.2.2 Capital Budgeting

As indicated in Table 3.1, capital funds are a large and important part of hospital budgeting. Capital funds are generated internally as well as provided by state and federal grants and sponsorship arrangements. Large-scale grant opportunities, including the $20 billion Medical Research Future Fund, support innovative investment in Australia. Treasury provides procurement policies, guidelines and strategic agendas drive large-scale investments, in particular digital health and technology investment. Risk analysis is a significantly important part of the Critical Infrastructure Act, which includes cybersecurity risk. Hospital electronic record systems (EMRs) are examples of costly digital health investments. Another recent example of a strategically important large-scale infrastructure project is the Victorian Heart Hospital, Australia's first dedicated cardiac hospital. Established in collaboration with Monash University, this means there is a tertiary hospital on university grounds, supporting research.

The models for smaller-scale investments are managed within hospitals to fund replacement equipment or new innovations that help reduce the cost of care. Funding can come from operational surplus, philanthropic donations, government initiatives or grant activity. The ad hoc approach and relationships with suppliers and research institutions potentially inhibits the innovative digital start-ups in this sector – many of which are clinicians solving local and specialised problems. Interviews with key players in this sector are required to understand how accounting can support innovation.

3.3 Operational Management and Budgeting Activities

Interviews with a range of stakeholders revealed some of the **capital expenditure issues.** For example, capital expenditure on technology and back-end functions are viewed with some cynicism and are **highly political** expenditure items. One of the interviewees claimed that while the $80–$90 million spent on EMRs is highly successful, the justifications are not easy to make. To begin, investments that are not bricks and mortar are not as appealing to sell to the electorate (as one interviewee said, *it's very hard for a minister to go and cut the ribbon on a medical health record*), as for example, the approximately $600 million Victorian Heart Hospital. Within the hospital, it was also suggested that philanthropic donations can contribute to internally generated investment pools, but donors also want their money to go to tangible investments, like medical equipment or clinical units. Investment in digital health medical records or accounting systems might not necessarily get internal funds or business case approval, even when justified from providing better patient quality outcomes. For the level of investment, they do not show much in the way of savings, especially when the fixed costs (around 70%) will not change. Nevertheless, as mentioned in the previous chapter, these valuation issues relate to the **short-term ROI vs the long-term VBHC returns** and staged benefits of a fully functioning digital health system need to be factored in. With fixed costs relating to salaries and infrastructure, this is not necessarily something that can be, or would want to be reduced. For example, interviewees in clinical coding confirmed that while their roles will not be lost, their roles will change because of digitised medical records. They will become more of a system auditor, a potentially more satisfying role. Even with higher levels of automation, the clinical coding role is challenging, and incumbents struggle to meet monthly activity-reporting reporting targets.

In terms of **preventative health investments**, representatives of the government funding body and a number of interviewees from different states all acknowledged that there is a big gap between hospitals investing in home-based care and receiving a dedicated funding stream, when it comes to virtual hospitals, and the more formal HITH. There is an argument that there is an enormous opportunity in remote monitoring, in keeping people out of hospital or reducing the number of admissions. This includes how technology is being used to keep people out of very expensive residential care for longer. Despite the opportunities, all interviewees see this aspect as a big challenge, with health services research still in its infancy, despite the wealth of data available. One innovative, that was not directly funded by the health department but was recognised as a strategically valuable intervention by the hospital CEO was a remote care digital service, set up by one hospital's HITH clinical directorate. The care intervention involves a two-tiered workforce health and social care model which utilises a non-healthcare frontline worker supported by a healthcare worker with the aim to keep high-risk patients out of hospital. The digital component of the model morphs together phone calls and service provision to a digital platform that uses AI to predict hospital admissions. The programme was set up as a long-term project to help provide a model of care with measured outcomes that could report back to the health department on the effectiveness of a VBHC approach. While this is not directly funded, the interviewees argued that, over time, they will need the finance and digital teams to work in conjunction with the model of care, in order to lobby government on its effectiveness and to ensure the programme will continue to exist and be correctly costed and assumed as part of government funding.

Several interviewees highlighted problems with grant opportunities which might provide initial start-up support, but longevity in funding sources becomes complicated. As such, there is a need for **sustainable business models**, with the expectation that other funders, such as health insurers and pharmaceutical companies, would be championing some of this activity too. One key interviewee suggested that Australian health insurers either do not think value-based health innovations will pay dividends yet or they cannot see the volume. Others argue that existing processes in Australia are not amenable to investment and that insurance companies do not have the incentive to support investment. One digital health company representative suggested that it is easier to start in the hospital setting and co-develop with the clinicians/users of the system in formal clinical trials (as they are doing in Singapore). They start with pharmaceutical companies to achieve a certain scale and work with overseas insurance companies to deploy the technology, as overseas insurers have clear benefits/dollar gains. Working with overseas investors helps with economic model studies. In the overseas examples, if clinical trials and business models are approved, the innovation is translated into action immediately in the same hospital. Whereas in Australia, investment approaches are less structured and involve partnering with universities before looking at commercialisation in the hospital setting. This was confirmed by a hospital administrator, who suggested that ad hoc problem-solving innovations do come from clinicians, but because of dedicated strategic agenda towards investing and the risk management impacts, the in-house initiatives might not fit and are harder to succeed without backing from big companies. While it appears that Australian hospitals are progressive and want change led by digital innovation, investment is stymied when taking a bottom-up approach (e.g., not taking a clinical trial approach or backed by significant external investment). Even if the latter occurs, the business models for ongoing translation within the sector do not necessarily work in an Australian environment. The regulatory environment, along with the inability to get access to the real decision-makers who have competing priorities, are arguably the greatest problems for innovative healthcare solutions.

From a **technical accounting perspective**, one interviewee mentioned the challenge of managing **growing levels of operating expenditure** and **reducing levels of capital expenditure**. The problem for the interviewee's hospital was defining investments in digital health as an asset. Once the infrastructure is in place, there is considerable ongoing expenditure in service provision, maintenance and support. The manager explained that the asset is 'data' which cannot be shared, sold or depreciated/amortised, resulting in data asset measurement challenges. With increased sophistication come associated procurement challenges. It was argued that there needs to be a changed mindset in what is deemed fit for market, contracting and vendor arrangements that are attuned to cybersecurity. There is a bigger role for using 'digital twin technology' (essentially, a testing sandpit) and for finance to become involved in providing advice on risks through a safe ecosystem/licensing arrangement embedded in business models. There is also an opportunity to better use this data and potentially share it for improved clinical outcome measurement and cost determination.

As raised in Chapter 2, the links between **measuring outcomes and linking these to funding models** were met with some concerns about how, or even if they should be incorporated. In moving to more substantive changes, it was suggested that one of the smaller states or regions could be used for pilot testing, but this is still future thinking. It was argued that the current stage is really about understanding the **variation in costs** across the jurisdictions. One interviewee was working on a project to understand the reason behind large variations between different hospitals. For example, one hospital has significantly longer ALOS for a particular DRG. What is the reason for this? Was it attributable to complications, sicker or older patients or coding irregularities? It appeared from the interviews that coding, although automated, is still reliant on the way medical records are written up. If a patient is admitted with one condition but ends up in intensive care on a ventilator for several days, then the more dominant DRG is used to fund the episode of care. From a medical forensic analysis perspective, the coding and detailed EMR can be used to track untoward events in order to look for errors or negligence. However, the power of the system has not yet been fully exploited in terms of data analysis and linking costs to outcomes.

From a costing perspective, the funding body argues that **Australia has a very robust costing system which is already bundling up episodes** and understanding the costs of care. However, others argue that it is not as easy in practice. For example, the obvious bundling activities are for inpatient activities, such as hip replacement or stroke with associated rehabilitation, or diabetes and multiple admissions over the course of a year. However, the **bundled payments are based on clinical and resource homogeneity**. This means that despite the fact that some patients require intensive rehabilitation and others minimal, all are coded under the one DRG. The **bundling does not differentiate** very well and is technically complex. As soon as multiple organisations become involved in the bundled payment, the single bundled payment needs to be separated out. Even in the one hospital there may be two organisations managing the same patient – one organisation for acute care and another for the rehabilitation stages. One interviewee explained this is where the system is stuck – that is, on **how to fund and resource heterogeneous patients**, rather than homogeneous ones.

It was argued by several interviewees that waste and non-value-added activities remain to be dealt with. At the same time, there is not enough recognition that low-cost items can have huge healthcare impacts. Interviewees argued that costs continue to be high and are associated with poor outcomes, without focusing enough on prevention and coordination that could keep people out of hospital. One example is diabetic amputation which is considered a failure in preventative care.

One aspect where the healthcare system is succeeding in terms of connecting accounting to clinicians is in regard to HACs, where there are the funding impacts if penalties are applied. These conditions were noted in Figure 3.2. HAC flags arguably provide a tool for clinicians and demonstrate that avoiding these saves money. A good example is 'falls'. Although not necessarily a HAC, falls have an impact on hospital admissions in general. One hospital representative explained how they had conducted a workshop on falls and discovered the hospital had approximately six different customer-facing services for people with falls, with each service operating as a silo and no information sharing. The interviewee discovered the hospital was unable to track customers who had falls, did not have a standardised pathway of care and did not have any ability to determine whether they were meeting patient needs. Based on current activity levels, the interviewee suggested that the hospital was not meeting current demand and that within five years demand was expected to double. With greater awareness of the potential to connect data and better manage resourcing, this interviewee provided a good example of a hospital VBHC activity that could result in keeping patients out of hospital.

Another area of interest is costly new medical and surgical interventions, some with price tags of up to a $1 million per patient. One interviewee explained that some expenditure items might provide a young person with vision for the rest of their life, but when is a treatment justified and when is it not? And how can personalised treatment be 'scaled up' to the point that it becomes cost-effective? Cancer therapies, for example, are already very expensive, with T-Cell therapy likely to become a first-line or second-line treatment, rather than a treatment of last resort, in the future. At what point is a treatment too expensive? These are questions that are difficult to answer, but more detailed analysis of direct and indirect costs can assist in providing further insights.

Box 3.1 Insights from Finland

Finland is currently working on a better understanding of episode-level costs. Health researchers have found that 10% of the population is responsible for 80% of the healthcare costs and even more surprisingly that 5% of the population is responsible for 57% of the costs (NHG, 2013). These are usually the patients who draw on multiple services, such as the elderly and people with mental health, and drug and alcohol issues. The integration of services for the 10% who use them the most is considered the most important area to address in social security reform policy and when planning freedom of choice. When it comes to the 5% of the population who dominate the use of social services, the need for integrated service provision becomes critical.

While Finland continues to use DRG-based costing in its hospitals, it is only used for measuring costs for one part of the patient pathway. The accounting resource is expanding beyond the hospital to episode-level accounting, involving primary and social care which previously had not been so interested in costs.

Like Australia, Finland is also facing rising treatment costs. Likewise, the Finnish government is similarly worried about being unable to afford cancer treatment in the future, as the population ages and cancer rates rise. However, in collecting longitudinal episode-level data, researchers noticed that the cost per cancer treatment has decreased despite more expensive medication and alternative technologies. Interestingly, the outcomes have also improved, along with reduced indirect costs, such as sick leave, early retirement and/or continued use of social resources. The reason for the change was due to standardisation of care, with big cancer groups (i.e., breast and prostate cancer) now being treated more on an outpatient basis.

Having VBHC protocols in place for 10 years, Finland has been able to follow patients over their entire episodes of care. With a separate cardiac hospital and five university hospitals, there is enough volume to build separate units, and research collaborations, to build on this wealth of data.

In conclusion, findings from the field interviews show that the major issues are fragmentation in the system, a lack of detailed data analysis around cost variations and the discontinuity of care between primary and secondary and hospital care. If these could be tackled with funding mechanisms around them, it would arguably be a 'game changer' for Australia.

3.4 Issues in Moving Toward VBHC

As highlighted in this chapter, there are several challenges with the current system that arguably require more detailed understanding of the costs and data that can be generated from the entire healthcare delivery system. Drawing on these findings, we have further adapted Table 3.3 to show how accountants can be supportive in the implementation of VBHC strategies, while considering the competing values of multiple stakeholders. Each is depicted in Table 3.3:

Table 3.3 A strategic values-based framework for VBHC implementation: ABF and appraisal

Strategy/Values	*How can accountants support?*
Measure health outcomes and costs Design solutions to improve health outcomes	Review the current ABF streams (including DRG-related funding models) and associated cost structures to focus on the opportunities for introducing bundled care arrangements (keeping patients out of hospital by delivering hospital in the home or on outpatient basis). Support investment appraisal and digital health investment with a strategic lens. Measure costs both direct and indirect, with the notion of indirect costs representing societal level costs (sick leave, early retirement and extended use of social resources). **Assist:** Strategically support initiatives that enable pilot testing of new solutions or ideas.
Industrial value	The system is recognising costly patient groupings but is working with complex government funding models. Exemplary hospital CEOs manage budgets with a comprehensive knowledge of costs and revenue streams. **Assist:** Ensure accountants are equipped with knowledge of costs and funding streams to support resource allocation and facilitate VBHC initiatives.
Market value	Digital health is recognised for its capacity to support long-term change. However, Australian healthcare systems are not maximising the potential for innovation and digital start-ups are developing their business models offshore. **Assist:** Improved evaluation methodologies, internal processes and collaborative partnerships to foster competition in innovation that reduces the cost of care.
Domestic value	Respected hospital CEOs and senior management are proactive in VBHC initiatives. **Assist:** Improved relationships can lead to generative VBHC activities and outcomes.
Civic value	The traditional DRG approach to costing activities is not being questioned. Understanding the rules of payment may lead to gaming or avoidance of service delivery. **Assist:** Improved understanding of the funding rules can provide scope for working with the government funders to legitimise pilot change initiatives.
Inspired value	Solutioning so far is clinically inspired and directed toward greater use of AI; accounting inspired value is stagnant in comparison. **Assist:** Provide improved support for accounting to move from a retrospective to a prospective co-producer.
Fame value	Non-tangible investments can be trapped by politics and need for public recognition. **Assist:** Accounting to influence public recognition through measurement.

3.5 Conclusion

In summary, this chapter contributes valuable insights into the intricate web of healthcare funding and investments in Australia, discussing challenges and opportunities and suggesting potential paths forward.

1 **Healthcare Payment Evolution:** This chapter makes contribution by diving into the intricate dynamics of Australia's approach to healthcare payments, emphasising the importance of bundled payments in achieving the aims of VBHC.
2 **Performance Evaluation and Healthcare Payments:** It contributes by bridging the gap between performance evaluation and healthcare payments by the government, shedding light on the decision-making process involved in allocating healthcare budgets and highlighting the significance of strategic investments in this sector.
3 **Activity-Based Funding:** An in-depth understanding of ABF is presented, elaborating on how hospitals are financed based on the number of weighted services they provide. The chapter contributes by providing insights into the advantages of ABF and explains how it encourages hospitals to maximise efficiency and effectiveness in their service delivery.
4 **Capital Budgeting in Healthcare:** Another contribution is that the role of capital funds in hospital budgeting is highlighted in this chapter. It points out how such funds can be generated internally and externally, through various means, including state and federal grants and fundings.
5 **Innovative Healthcare Investment:** The chapter contributes by unveiling various innovative healthcare investments in Australia, like the Victorian Heart Hospital. It also touches upon the challenges and opportunities in funding these innovations and the need for sustainable healthcare business models.
6 **Challenges of Digital Health Investments:** The chapter delves deep into the problems faced by the healthcare sector in adopting digital health investments. It discusses the issues related to defining such investments as assets and the associated challenges in terms of procurement, service provision, maintenance and support.
7 **The Role of Health Insurers and Overseas Investors:** It explains the seeming hesitation of Australian health insurers in investing in value-based health innovations and contrasts the investment models in Australia with those in other countries, like Finland and Singapore.
8 **Interview Insights:** This chapter is enriched by various interviews with stakeholders, revealing real-world challenges and perspectives on capital expenditure, innovative healthcare solutions and the current funding scenario.
9 **Technical Accounting Challenges:** This chapter touches upon the technical accounting challenges faced by hospitals, particularly regarding managing operating and capital expenditure. The chapter delves into the conceptual challenges of defining and managing 'data' as an asset.

10 **Risk Management and Cybersecurity:** With the increasing shift towards digital solutions, the chapter underscores the importance of considering risks associated with cybersecurity. It advocates for the need for a changed mindset in terms of market readiness, contracting and vendor arrangements.
11 **Recommendations for Improved Outcomes and Cost Determination:** Building on the insights and challenges discussed, the chapter suggests potential opportunities for better utilisation and sharing of data to achieve improved clinical outcomes and cost determinations.

In conclusion, this chapter highlights four key takeaways for accountants to proactively support value-based investment and funding model change.

Key Takeaway 1: Have a detailed understanding of the costs and revenue streams to provide strategic insights.

Key Takeaway 2: Support investment appraisal in digital health with well-executed risk management strategies that do not stifle innovation. Consider incentives that support greater investment by insurers, pharma and aligned organisations.

Key Takeaway 3: Be prepared to engage in extensive AI predictive analytics for clinical forecasting and cost management activities.

Key Takeaway 4: Work on partnerships that foster accounting as a proactive co-producer of change.

References

Australian Institute of Health and Welfare. (2022). *Digital health.* Australian Government Department of Health and Aged Care. Retrieved December 5, 2022, from https://www.aihw.gov.au/reports/australias-health/digital-health

Bennett, C. C. (2009). A healthier future for all Australians: An overview of the final report of the National Health and Hospitals Reform Commission. *Medical journal of Australia*, *191*(7), 383–387. 10.5694/j.1326-5377.2009.tb02845.x

Independent Health and Aged Care Pricing Authority. (2022). NWAU calculators. Retrieved December 5, 2022, from https://www.ihacpa.gov.au/health-care/pricing/nwau-calculators

Lichkus, J., Wolf, C., Hynds, R., Moorer, K., Bourgoine, D., Garabedian, N., & Eamranond, P. (2019). Effect of implementing a bundled-payment program for heart failure at a safety-net community hospital. *Population Health Management*, *22*(1), 12–18. 10.1089/pop.2018.0001

Maru, C., Lin, A., Kagubare, K., Pollack, A., Stern, A., Rao, N., & Walker, J. (2019). *Leapfrog to Value: How nations can adopt value-based care on the path to universal health coverage*. Leapfrog to Value. https://static1.squarespace.com/static/5db772d44638535b2114f2e6/t/5ddea52751c72e2c5edacd77/1574872363413/2019_LeapfrogToValue.pdf

Miao, Y., Yuan, X., Gu, J., Zhang, L., He, R., Sandeep, S., & Wu, J. (2019). Constructing a value-based healthcare system for hypertensive patients through changing payment mode: Evidence from a comparative study in rural China. *Journal of Medical Economics*, 22(3), 245–251. 10.1080/13696998.2018.1558864

4 Health Information Systems in Value-Based Healthcare

Say Yen Teoh, Malshika Dias, Gillian Vesty, Miia Jansson, Tarek Rana, and Kerryn Butler-Henderson

4.1 Introduction

The global digital health industry is estimated to be worth more than $550 billion by 2027 (Mulcahy, 2022). Along with 5 billion worldwide internet users and 67% with mobile devices (Dive-Reclus and Jaeger, 2022), digital health has the potential for improvement across the sector, including greater patient access to care, data analytics for enhanced medical diagnoses and clinical decisions, digital therapeutics, wearable devices for remote monitoring and self-management, as well as data exchange and information systems for improved accounting and clinical administration. Technology is at the forefront of delivering value-based healthcare (VBHC) and measuring performance outcomes (Porter and Teisberg, 2006; Teisberg et al., 2020; Sicilia, 2022). Contemporary digital health including the most advanced technologies, such as virtual and augmented reality, sensors, telemedicine and robotics, can support preventive, predictive, personalised and participatory care, transforming traditional modes of healthcare delivery.

4.2 Health Information Systems and Emerging Technologies

Health Information Systems (HIS) are defined as 'systems that capture, store, manage, and transmit information related to the health of individuals or the activities of organisations that work within the healthcare sector' (World Health Organization, 2021). HIS has the potential to improve patient care, increase efficiency and reduce costs. HIS can also facilitate data sharing and decision-making among healthcare providers, researchers and policymakers. In addition, HIS is argued to enable better care and outcomes at a lower cost by allowing hospitals and health systems to share medical equipment across facilities (Nabelsi and Gagnon, 2017).

Countries around the world have invested heavily in developing their own HIS infrastructure. In Australia, the government has implemented a national eHealth strategy aimed at establishing a secure and interoperable HIS that supports the delivery of safe and efficient healthcare services (Department of Health, 2022). The My Health Record system is one such initiative that

DOI: 10.4324/9781032685489-4

allows patients to access and share their health information with healthcare providers. The Australian Digital Health Agency (ADHA) provides leadership in the implementation and adoption of HIS (ADHA, 2022) which contributes somewhat to the movement towards VBHC. Since the COVID-19 pandemic, the Australian healthcare system has shifted its ongoing investment into developing and implementing new technologies to create a more agile and responsive healthcare system to deliver value-based services throughout Australia (Jones et al., 2023). For example, telehealth, electronic prescriptions and home delivery of medications were made possible under the Medicare Benefits Schedule due to COVID-19 (MBS Online, 2022).

In early 2022, the Australian government announced an investment of A$107.2 million to modernise Australian healthcare systems. This included introducing innovative digital health services and streamlining healthcare payments so that more health services will be made available digitally, including Medicare enrolment and re-enrolment, and the written authority of the Pharmaceutical Benefits Scheme services (Jones et al., 2023). The recent developments of digital health technology and services in Australia include the following:

- **Electronic prescribing** – An alternative to paper prescriptions for healthcare professionals, pharmacies and patients to use.
- **Medicare online** – A portal to claim, update and access health statements.
- **COVID-19 Vaccine Clinic Finder** – A one-stop-shop national portal providing a complete list of all clinics in Australia which allows consumers to compare clinics, check availability and book an appointment.
- **Secure messaging** – Allows the secure, encrypted exchange of clinical information between health professionals.
- **COVID-19 digital certificates** – Digital access for the proof of COVID-19 vaccination in Australia.
- **My Health Record** – A secure digital health platform where summary health information can be stored and accessed by Australians and their authorised healthcare providers. If data has been kept up to date, it can provide a complete summary of an individual's health, and it is available 24/7 (Australian Institute of Health and Welfare, 2022). Chamonix was awarded $2.1 million to support the eHealth record with a consumer-facing mobile app. My Health Record is FHIR (Fast Health Interoperability Resources)-compliant, drawing data from other information systems and requiring two-factor authentication through a myGov account to access (Hendry, 2021). It is a personally controlled record, as the individual controls who can access their record and sections in their record.

There are different levels of HIS from digital versions of a patient's record used for internal purposes – e.g., by clinicians for diagnosis and treatment records – to more cloud-based systems where data is shared between providers. According to Healthcare Information and Management Systems Society (HIMSS), the different HIS include the following:

Electronic Medical Record (EMR) – An electronic record of health-related information on an individual that can be created, gathered, managed and consulted by authorised clinicians and staff within one healthcare organisation.

Electronic Health Record (EHR) –An electronic record of health-related information on an individual that conforms to nationally recognised interoperability standards and that can be created, managed and consulted by authorised clinicians and staff across more than one healthcare organisation (Healthcare Information and Management Systems Society [HIMSS], 2020).

Typically, the difference between EHRs and EMRs is how holistic the system is and what organisations are contributing to the data within the system. The terms Clinical Information Systems (CIS), EMR and EHR are frequently used interchangeably, especially as cloud-based functionality develops. Cerner and Epic are the most dominant EMRs in the larger teaching hospitals in Australia and are usually single-site implementations (see Figure 4.1 for details). Allscripts and InterSystems are also used, while Covio is the largest telehealth provider in Australia. In primary care, the most popular EMRs are Best Practice, Medical Director and ZedMed.

Australian hospitals also use a range of HIS to support clinical information VBHC efforts. Dominant in the market are Oracle's Cerner (25% market share) and Epic (33% market share). In Australia both Epic and Cerner are used throughout the country, with Epic winning the NSW Health contract over incumbent Cerner. Epic is also used in the ACT and the Royal Melbourne

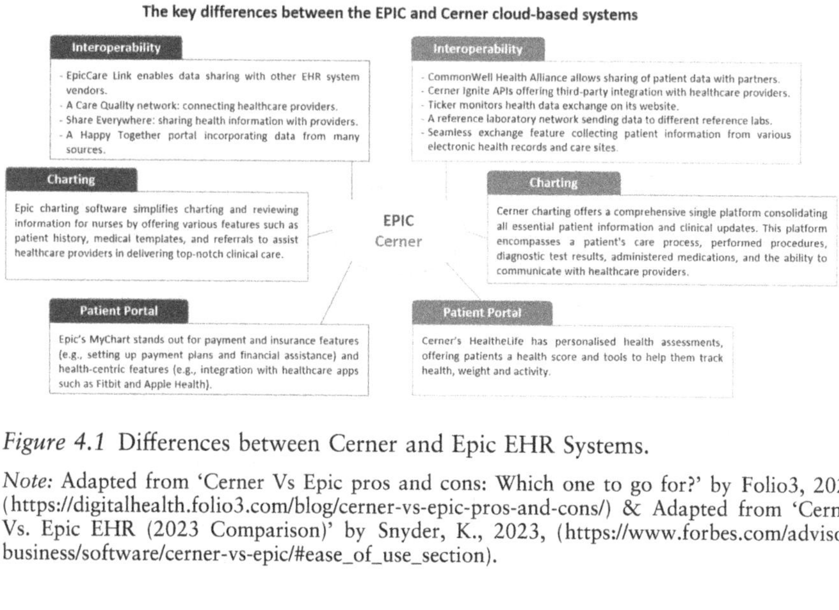

Figure 4.1 Differences between Cerner and Epic EHR Systems.

Note: Adapted from 'Cerner Vs Epic pros and cons: Which one to go for?' by Folio3, 2023 (https://digitalhealth.folio3.com/blog/cerner-vs-epic-pros-and-cons/) & Adapted from 'Cerner Vs. Epic EHR (2023 Comparison)' by Snyder, K., 2023, (https://www.forbes.com/advisor/business/software/cerner-vs-epic/#ease_of_use_section).

Hospital, Victoria. Other hospitals in Victoria and Queensland use Cerner. The key differences between the cloud-based systems are outlined in Figure 4.1.

Both systems aim to support VBHC by enabling healthcare providers to access patient information in real-time, including medical history, medications and test results, allowing for more accurate and timely diagnoses and treatment plans (Sicilia, 2022). By leveraging these systems, healthcare providers in Australia can improve patient outcomes, reduce costs and enhance the overall quality of care.

Nevertheless, the implementation of HIS faces challenges such as data privacy and security, interoperability and user acceptance (Jansson et al., 2022a). Varying approaches are proposed including stakeholder engagement, standardisation and governance (Fernández-Alemán et al., 2013). Concerns about security and privacy of health data in a digital environment are among the significant challenges faced (Kushniruk et al., 2019). Furthermore, the fragmented nature of Australia's HIS has highlighted the need for better integration of digital health technologies into clinical workflows.

To support the digital health movement, many government-led initiatives have been aimed at encouraging private investment in digital health and driving innovation in this sector. The integration of AI and other cutting-edge technologies, such as the Internet of Things (IoT), data analytics, machine-learning, robotics and virtual reality, is rapidly transforming the landscape of digital health. For example, the federal Early-Stage Venture Capital Limited Partnerships Program has raised new venture capital funds between $10 million and $200 million (Australian Taxation Office, 2023) with the aim of offering value-based delivery (Jones et al., 2023). Some of these initiatives are now detailed in the following subsections.

4.2.1 *AI in Healthcare*

Investing in AI for prevention and management can help shift the focus of healthcare from reactive to preventive care. These tools have opened new possibilities for health services, enabling the development of innovative interventions that improve patient monitoring, disease detection, prevention and management (Rowlands, 2019). These tools can contribute to VBHC by improving efficiency, reducing errors and personalising treatment. For example, AI can help in the early detection of diseases and predicting patient outcomes, leading to better prevention and management of chronic diseases. AI can also aid in decision-making by providing physicians with real-time insights and recommendations based on a patient's unique characteristics and medical history (Jansson et al., 2022b). In addition, AI can help reduce healthcare costs and improve patient outcomes by identifying high-risk patients and providing targeted interventions. This can result in better care coordination, improved patient experience and reduced healthcare expenses.

In Figure 4.2, an example of a data landscape for predictive modelling of hospital-acquired infections (HAI) is provided. The diagram highlights

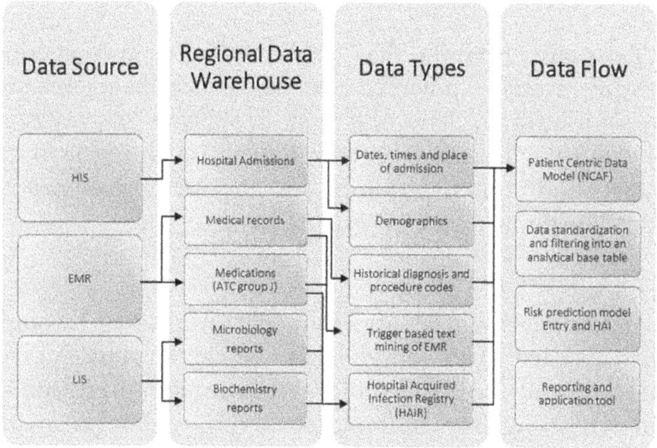

Figure 4.2 Data Landscape for Predictive Modelling of Hospital Acquired Infections.

Note: Adapted from 'Prediction of risk of acquiring urinary tract infection during hospital stay based on machine-learning: A retrospective cohort study' by Møller, J. K., Sørensen, M., & Hardahl, C., 2021, *Plos One*, *16*(3), p. 4 (https://doi.org/10.1371/journal.pone.0248636). Copyright © 2021 by Plos One.

connections to the Laboratory Information System (LIS) reports that build a narrative for predictive modelling and reporting. The data landscape includes links between the hospital Health Information System (HIS), electronic medical records (EMRs) and LIS, which trace the microbiology and biochemistry reports to HAIs as part of risk prediction modelling. The authors of the study specifically used the HIS system for prediction of risk of acquiring urinary tract infection during hospital stay based on machine-learning (Møller et al., 2021). Frondelius et al. (2022) also explored the AI predictions of patients in intensive care who acquired ventilator-assisted pneumonia. There are numerous studies by clinicians in AI prediction beginning to dominate the literature, providing accounting insights into the potential for more detailed analysis around the cost of managing these health risks as well as supporting the move to standardised pathways of care.

In mid-2022, one of the world's largest medical diagnostics provided a joint venture with Sonic Healthcare to develop and commercialise AI solutions in pathology. Artrya Limited raised $40 million to develop AI-based software solutions for non-invasive diagnosis of coronary artery disease including a software-as-a-medical-device service (Jones et al., 2023).

While the development of AI innovation in Australian healthcare is still in its early stages, there are promising signs of growth and investment. The government, academic institutions and private companies are all investing in research and development of AI technologies to improve healthcare outcomes.

So far, there are a total of 122 AI-based healthcare start-ups in Australia (Tracxn, 2022).

Recently, Sydney Adventist Hospital has implemented a cutting-edge early-warning monitoring system, powered by AI, which helps ensure patients remain safe and healthy. It is the first healthcare provider in Australia to use this real-time system for every patient, enabling staff to intervene before patient conditions deteriorate and they require intensive care (Australian Private Hospitals Association, 2022).

4.2.2 Remote Patient Monitoring

Australia's shift towards empowering the service model in healthcare through digital technologies has also led to the development of the **Remote Patient Monitoring (RPM)** collaboration tool. This tool allows care teams to remotely monitor inpatients and outpatients from multiple locations by connecting with wearable health technology. The RPM device delivers data continually to a medical team, allowing them to automatically intervene if there is a change that requires attention, such as a pacemaker adjustment or a medication modification. Connectivity through mobile apps combined with wearable health technologies contributes to a seamless delivery of care, enabling people to live their lives with greater confidence and less worry. Such digital innovation has revolutionised the healthcare sector, empowering people of all ages to take control of their health and well-being.

Additionally, RPM allows for better tracking of patient healthcare data once they are discharged, as it can collate a wide range of data such as vital signs, blood pressure, blood oxygen levels, blood sugar, heart rate and electrocardiograms. This tool does not require interactive video communication and is not restricted to a specific area. With RPM, patients can use a mode of technology that aggregates and interprets physiological data, such as a blood pressure cuff that wirelessly connects to a phone app and transmits the data to the patient's physician for analysis. Advanced cloud-sharing platforms and dedicated patient portals also allow healthcare professionals and patients to manage and share varied health data. Large mainstream technology companies, including Google, Apple and Amazon, have recognised the potential of the RPM market, leading to significant changes in healthcare.

RPM technologies have increased quality of life for patients, reduced hospitalisations and shortened hospital stays. Many companies are introducing and upgrading RPM devices, and the interest of technology giants in RPM will lead to the increased availability of clinical-grade wearables, improved connectivity and continued miniaturisation of devices for home use. Although there is a growing market for RPM technologies, simplification of connection technologies will be critical for broader adoption. Currently, approximately 88% of Australian hospitals and health systems have invested in or plan to invest in RPM technologies as part of their transition to a value-based care model, which aims to improve the quality of patient care while reducing costs (O'Luanaigh and Hutchison, 2020; Wells, 2022).

4.2.3 Managing the Package of Emerging Digital Technologies

Together this digital health package has significantly improved healthcare quality and effectiveness while lowering the costs for service providers, patients and enabling greater access for clinical research. These disruptive technologies have also resulted in patient empowerment (Hägglund et al., 2022). Patients are not solely reliant on individual medical professionals to dictate their healthcare choices now there is a growing sophistication of connectivity, accessibility and personalised medicine refining decision-making towards quality-measured, integrated care. Such digital empowerment has begun to revolutionise the healthcare sector (Reis et al., 2018).

Although exciting, there are inhibiting factors to the adoption of digital healthcare. Digital healthcare needs to be accessible, equitable and affordable for end-users, while also enhancing efficiency, strengthening health promotion and protecting patient information. Moreover, governments and institutions need to provide sufficient support and investment to encourage the adoption of digital health and improved digital literacy. At present, the Australian digital healthcare system integration is still emerging. There remains a conflict between a health system that puts people first by giving patients more choice, control and transparency versus one that provides seamless and coordinated care for patients. As health systems continue to transform, mentorship, financial support and effective management are necessary to promote change. Ultimately, digital health needs to be governed by ethical and secure practices and developed with transparent, accessible and confidential principles (Australia's National Digital Health Strategy, 2020).

All in all, the complex nature of VBHC requires extensive and continued investigation, especially as the 'value' of digital health interventions is informed by trends, evolution, evidence-based medicine and the changing population needs. Trends emerge as information flows evolve. This can also inform and transform the concept of 'value', with new barriers and constraints in the adoption of digital health continually emerging in the transition to VBHC.

4.3 Accounting for Digital Health

From an accounting perspective, there remain several challenges to improve healthcare services and foster the move to VBHC. First, the significant aspect raised by HIS interviewees was **data security**. Second, the accountant interviewees raised the importance of **understanding the systems and the data flows**. Third, the senior hospital managers explained the challenges with **investment appraisal and the disparity** between what is possible and demanded by clinicians and where the system currently lets them down.

4.3.1 Understanding the Security of Data

Access to digital health services requires health information to be confidential, secure and protected from cyber criminals and unauthorised access. Privacy and information sharing have become increasingly important topics in today's digital world. When it comes to information flows, it is essential to maintain a balance between the extent of information sharing and related privacy concerns. The HIS managers have explained the governance requirements on them and how the country-level and state-level governments have introduced Personal Information Protection (PIP) Acts to address privacy concerns. Cyber and IT security has recently become a growing concern in the Australian healthcare industry. As healthcare systems become increasingly digitised, the risk of cyber-attacks and data breaches has risen. In 2019, the ADHA reported that healthcare was the top industry sector impacted by data breaches, accounting for 54% of all breaches reported to the Office of the Australian Information Commissioner (ADHA, 2019). As such, building trust with patients and other stakeholders is important, and this can be achieved by prioritising patient privacy and complying with relevant regulations. Hence, integrating information flow and protecting patient privacy are critical elements of value-based care services. By prioritising the accuracy and security of patient data and complying with relevant regulations, Australians can receive high-quality care while maintaining their confidence in the healthcare system.

The importance of standardising and integrating information systems was raised by interviewees as essential, as this means the data can be stored on the same platform. Standardisation improves the accuracy and completeness of patient data. This is not only to improve data analytics and improve on number of errors or any inefficiencies in the delivery of healthcare services, but also to ensure that data is contained in a single place for security purposes, making cyber threats and data breaches easier to detect and respond to. A recent Australian Strategic Policy Institute report notes that 'cybersecurity is not just about technology; it is also about people, processes, and governance' (Australian Strategic Policy Institute, 2021). This was evident in interviews, where interviewees from some institutions spoke about taking a comprehensive approach to governance that includes technical measures such as firewalls and encryption and the development of policies and procedures to promote best practices in data management and privacy. They also explained the strict compliance mechanisms required when evaluating new technologies and noted that support from accounting would be vital in helping identify and manage risks. Compliance also made the organisation risk adverse when it came to evaluating new initiatives.

Another HIS manager from a different institution shared that there is not enough emphasis on IT security and auditing in the clinical information systems. This manager explained the important monitoring role that her team performed, but in general she felt that there was still not enough attention on IT security. The interviewee explained that governance processes in the PIP Act are relatively immature, mentioning that many do not understand the circumstances in which PIP applies and how to go about sharing data, and whether it needs to be de-identified. There are concerns that *people still do not know how to correctly de-identify and safely transmit data.* The interviewee complained it was individuals, like them who managed their own systems through audits and removing any clinical ID user who had not logged into the system for six months. They do surveillance auditing on health records and random confidentiality audits and audits for emergency access for My Health Record but argued that there is not enough security auditing. They are all given cybersecurity training, but not putting it into action through explicit IT security auditing and *making sure people are doing the right thing*. Thus, education of service providers who have access to the data is essential.

Although the Australian Digital Health Agency notes that 'effective interoperability and data sharing are key enablers for improving health outcomes and enabling innovation' (ADHA, 2019). The evidence from Finland shows that that country is further ahead than Australia. However, the overall sense is that Australian health providers are not yet ready or confident to get to this stage. Interviewees from tech companies and digital health start-ups all recognised this problem – stagnation towards innovation and some reticence to take risks. Nevertheless, once the staged investment in digital health moves beyond the current stage, confidence in having system interoperability for data sharing will grow.

Box 4.1 Insights from Finland

In 2018, the ***General Data Protection Regulation (GDPR)*** *was enacted across the EU. In 2019, a separate law on the secondary use of health and social data (*https://stm.fi/en/secondary-use-of-health-and-social-data) was enacted in Finland. *The purpose of the* ***Act on the Secondary Use of Health and Social Data*** *(552/2019) is to facilitate the effective and safe processing and access to the personal health and social data for scientific research, statistics,* ***development, and innovation activities****, steering and supervision, planning and reporting, teaching, and knowledge management.*

Findata is the Finnish Social and Health Data Permit Authority, which grant permits for the secondary use of health and social data (https://findata.fi/en/). *In addition, Findata is responsible for combining and pre-processing the data which is subject to a permit, such as the production of pseudonymised and anonymised statistical data from numerous public health and social sector controllers, registration of data from private healthcare and social welfare organisers, and saving customer data in the Patient Data Repository* (https://www.kanta.fi/en/professionals/patient-data-repository).

Data that is subject to data permits and amendment permits can only be analysed in an environment that meets specific requirements. Kapseli® is a Findata-provided secure operating environment for the processing of data on individuals. At the same time, the majority of the patient information systems in clinical use (Incl administrative registers) have been integrated into the data lakes for scientific research, leadership support, and international cooperation to support both primary and secondary use of health and social data.

Open data has significant social, economic, and environmental value for different stakeholders. ***According to the preliminary report on the effects of the secondary use of health and social data,*** *however, the 2019 Act* ***has not yet achieved its full potential*** *in research, development, innovation, and teaching activities* (Gesund Partners, 2022). *The key perspectives of the open data and its usability are outlined in* Figure 4.3.

Figure 4.3 Opposing Perspectives of Closed and Open Data.

Note: Adapted from 'Esiselvitys toisiolain vaikutuksista sote-tietojen toisiokäyttöön tutkimus-, kehitys- ja innovaatiotoiminnassa sekä opetuksessa' by Gesund Partners, 2022 (https://findata.fi/wp-content/uploads/sites/13/2022/02/Esiselvitys-toisiolain-vaikutuksista-sote-tietojen-toisiokayttoon-tutkimus-kehitys-ja-innovaatiotoiminnassa-seka-opetuksessa.pdf). Copyright © 2021 by Gesund Partners.

4.3.2 Understanding Information Flows

For the accountant, it is important to understand the information flows for accessing and connecting appropriate digital health channels and stakeholders. Interviewees explained that systems ranged from paper-based digitised inputs to more comprehensive systems with thousands of users that all connect through to the 'My Health Record'. However, they all agree information flows between different systems could still be improved. There are many inefficient workflows between different stakeholders, departments and systems of the healthcare services.

Connectivity between healthcare providers is important as public hospitals undertake outsourcing activities to specialist units and contract surgical procedures and medical beds to private hospitals to help manage throughput. Also, because of the complex funding arrangements, any contracted or bundled activity needs to be separated and transferred to the correct cost centre, contracting individual or institution. For example, when patients are transferred to Hospital in the Home (HITH) beds the funding remains within the hospital, but there is important connectivity required between treating clinicians, HITH staff, the patient's GP as well as the patient themselves and their family. Several interviewees mentioned the important partnerships and information connectivity that serves to build relationships and streamline patient care pathway. Despite the increasing adoption of EMRs by the large teaching hospitals and healthcare providers, there are still many health services, including private hospitals that do not have digital health capabilities. It is not a business case for some institutions who do not have the financial capacity. Other institutions, who do have the digital capability are arguing that they still manually manage their information transfers to other institutions, for example, from public to private hospitals, through written and photocopied records. These facilities have the electronic delivery capacity, but the receiving facility is not well equipped. Even some larger hospitals are not equipped for receiving remote patient ECGs or external urine or blood tests as they cannot be electronically uploaded to a system for sharing.

The inefficiency is quite frustrating, particularly when the potential for integration and mass predictive data analytics is within reach. The GPs interviewed complained that they did not know when their patients were being discharged or even when they were being treated through HITH. They relied on the patients, rather than the hospital, to contact them. As indicated in Chapter 3, this disconnect could be a function of the funding models and debates over who should bear the cost burden, but it is also a demonstration of a system that is not fully integrated and automated. For the elderly and chronically ill, the lack of integration is a costly and potentially life-threating problem. While innovation in improved remote monitoring, predictive analytics and connectivity capacity for continuity of care is possible with the available products and can be customised to some extent, the current digital medical record in a majority of institutions is simply an electronic version of the paper record and does not necessarily provide better patient care. Interviewees revealed there are local innovations occurring. But these are often funded internally, by proactive CEOs who have a longer-term strategic view.

The design of healthcare systems varies depending on the vendor. Some vendors prioritise customising the system to fit the healthcare needs, while others prioritise design that matches the workflow. Most interviewees described the need for funding for future systems, designed with the primary goal of providing the best patient care, rather than just reporting statistics. One of the senior accountants interviewed explained that this is the most important aspect – *understand the data* – that is, to employ a systems-thinking mindset to be able to provide strategic advice and to use the EMRs to their upmost capacity while the staged upgrades and more powerful predictive capabilities are still in the pipeline. Knowing what to ask the data is essential. Unfortunately, interviewees claim accounting in hospitals can be invisible with too many providing data as reports on past performance. The clinical coders interviewed did not know the accounting/finance team, or even where they were located or how their systems connected. Silos of expertise remain, and the future-focused strategic management accountant is not so readily found, which appeared to be a problem for many interviewees.

With next steps underway in some jurisdictions, improving information flows through system integration will create significant value for different stakeholders in the healthcare system. Healthcare providers can improve efficiency, enhance communication and reduce medical errors by establishing connections between information systems. This can result in better data management and analytics, improving outcomes and higher patient satisfaction. Overall, smooth information flows can help healthcare organisations provide more effective and efficient care while also optimising resource utilisation and identifying areas for improvement.

4.3.3 Investment in Digital Health

Access to investment funds comes from several sources. Discussions with hospital executives suggest that funds for digital health investment within hospitals come from:

- **Internal funding** (as a result of capital funds from operating expenditure and philanthropic donations)
- **Research grants**
- **Government initiatives**

There appears to be a certain degree of autonomy for CEOs and executive teams to operate with an investment-centre mindset, even though significant funding is based on cost reimbursement. A cost activity-matching mindset was argued to be detrimental to investment and innovation, with several interviewees noting the importance of senior management in supporting technological innovation and long-term change.

At the clinical level, innovations in remote medicine (e.g., remote ECGs attended to immediately by trained cardiologists at major hospitals, telehealth to individuals and elderly patients in nursing homes and increased admissions to HITH) have dramatically increased. This is largely due to the COVID-19 pandemic. Other innovations, such as predictive modelling and early-warning checks on the potential for disease conditions, or requirement for intervention/treatment based on EMR data are still in early trials. Primary care and HIS managers are experiencing a growth in this area, with requests for expenditure from their own in-house clinical designers, as well as from digital start-ups and recipients of seed funding and large corporates. As one HIS executive stated: *The clinicians want it and they're ready for it. But we haven't caught up yet.* Some clinical and administrative interviewees shared publications of the AI predictive modelling that they have been involved in, highlighting the enthusiasm in this space.

From an accounting perspective, the HIS managers and executive procurement teams require support on how to properly evaluate these emerging innovations, as well as how to manage/rank the competing priorities, especially when there are powerful healthcare stakeholders all vying for scarce resources. As indicated earlier, the risk is relatively high on the cyber and data security perspective, but there are a number of factors that also need to be considered, such as financial outlay and ongoing maintenance costs (which are frequently higher than the initial outlay), reputable vendor, system compatibility and flexibility, ease of use and system training, internal/government governance process requirements, etc. Together, these provide appraisal and cost-benefit analysis challenges, for not necessarily agile organisations. The significant requirements for HIS investment appraisal, such as seeking approvals and obtaining funding, mean that procurement is a slow process. Meanwhile technological advances are rapidly multiplying while some earlier investments are becoming outdated. Looping back to the earlier section, this is also where it is essential that the accountant understand the data and data flows to provide strategic insights into what is priority for the institution.

The integration of digital innovations such as AI into a larger healthcare system could lead to VBHC, which focuses on improving patient outcomes while reducing costs. For example, AI-powered disease detection and diagnosis could lead to earlier detection of diseases, more accurate diagnoses and personalised treatment plans, which could in turn result in improved patient outcomes and reduced healthcare costs in the long term. However, the full potential of these AI innovations in generating VBHC will depend on how well they are integrated into existing healthcare systems and how effectively they are able to improve patient outcomes while reducing costs. The integration of AI and other advanced technologies need long-term collaborations between healthcare providers and technology companies. Healthcare providers can benefit from partnering with technology start-ups to develop innovative applications not only based on the current needs of their patients but also considering preventative care towards generating VBHC.

In conclusion, the integration of technology in healthcare requires a significant shift in how clinical and administrative professionals work and communicate with each other, and this shift must be supported by comprehensive education and training programmes. Interviewees suggest that there is a broad range of technical capabilities from those who are tech-savvy to those who want everything to remain as it has been. All agree, however, that they want the healthcare environment to be more efficient. Interviewees from some of the smaller states noted that, whenever they travelled interstate, or overseas, and then returned to their own hospital, it felt like they were 'going back in time'. This highlights the disparity in the system, which is slowly connecting through strategic investment. It has been noted on numerous occasions that the COVID-19 pandemic supported a technology uplift. Those who resisted change altogether are now saying, *Okay, that might work.*

For the accountant, there are key insights drawn from the interviews that include a deeper understanding of the information flows and value of data that is generated by the varying systems. There are important strategic decisions on data governance risks and management of safe ecosystems, along with associated risks when investing in digital health technologies. These need to be considered in investment appraisal and when ranking competing demands for emerging systems and clinical interventions. Further, the accountant needs to operate as a finance business partner.

4.4 Implications for VBHC

Given the highly specialised nature of digital health and the digital health expertise that is available to work closely with the management accountants, it is important to understand how HIS professionals can support information flows, which will in turn make data collection easier for accountants. Table 4.1 provides an overview of the important activities that foster strategic information flows in a healthcare setting.

Based on the analysis above, Table 4.2 summarises the aspects to consider when attempting to further improve healthcare information flows in delivering value-based care.

Table 4.1 How can HIS professionals improve healthcare information flows?

Strategic information flows	*How can information systems professionals help?*
Health information system design	• Design the health information system to enable seamless information sharing and effective decision-making across stakeholders in VBHC. • Design a system that incorporates user-centred design principles, interoperability with other systems and high-quality data to improve the accuracy and completeness of the information flowing through the system.
Streamline workflows for optimal performance	• Streamline workflows of healthcare systems in a way that reduces the risk of errors, delays and redundancies that can compromise the quality of care. • Analyse workflows and implement automation and decision support tools to improve the efficiency of information flows and enhance the value of the care delivery.
Privacy and information sharing	• Develop necessary policies and procedures by each healthcare stakeholder, in addition to government or state policies, to protect patient privacy and ensure secure information sharing. • Implement policies, procedures and security measures prioritising privacy and compliance with relevant regulations to improve the accuracy and completeness of the information flowing through the systems. • Enable a digital environment where patients feel confident that their data is being used appropriately by communicating the policies and measures in place.

(*Continued*)

Table 4.1 (Continued)

Strategic information flows	*How can information systems professionals help?*
Cyber and IT security	• Introduce strong security measures such as multi-factor authentication, firewalls, and intrusion detection systems to prevent data breaches and protect the value of the care being delivered. • Implement mechanisms to protect the integrity of the information flowing through the system to ensure that malicious actors do not compromise it. • Educate healthcare staff regarding cyber-attacks and how to prevent them in practice.
Upskilling healthcare workforce	• Improve digital literacy of healthcare providers on using technology to reduce waiting times, access appropriate information and manage data more effectively. • Upskill workforce on data management techniques to ensure that the data is accurate, complete and available when needed, improving the efficiency of care delivery. • Enhance analytics skills to help healthcare workers identify trends, monitor patient health in real time and improve value-based outcomes through early and timely diagnosis. • Educate healthcare workers regarding ethical and secure use of information to minimise human error when managing confidential data.
Other types of digital innovations	• Integrate HIS with other digital innovations such as artificial intelligence (AI), telemedicine and data analytics to advance the information flowing through the system and deliver better value. • Enable more targeted interventions, personalised care, and real-time patient health monitoring to improve outcomes and reduce costs.

Table 4.2 A strategic values-based framework for VBHC implementation

Strategy/Values	*How can accountants support?*
Design solutions to improve health outcomes	Detail digital infrastructure **risk management, data flows** and **digital health investment** appraisal activities. **Assist:** Engagement with HIS expertise to understand the data flows and resource implications from a budgeting and performance evaluation perspective.
Industrial value	The focus on costs and efficiency has taken a backseat as innovation and regulatory justifications follow inspired value and those associated with civic responsibility. Nevertheless, there is a long-term approach which fits within

(*Continued*)

Table 4.2 (Continued)

Strategy/Values	*How can accountants support?*
	the remit of industrial value which regards decision-making for the longevity of operations. Standardisation of data flows supports efficient and secure systems. **Assist:** Ensure the efficiency focus does not get overrun by clinical/administrative and political power struggles for new innovations. Work to standardise data flows for efficient and secure outcomes.
Market value	The market is alive with innovative digital health technologies with multiple players, such as clinicians, tech companies, pharma (start-up as well as mature) competing with solutions for both administrative and clinical purposes. **Assist:** Support with appraisal tools that enable fair, transparent but strategic evaluations and ranking to key priorities.
Domestic value	There are powerful players in the healthcare setting. Governance processes are a mechanism to keep people in check. In the HIS area, these safeguards help secure the system. **Assist:** Translating HIS education and training around solutioning; accounting to be a co-producer.
Civic value	Regulatory oversight is critical in the HIS field, where there is major risk for data breaches and potential cyber impacts. Regulation in this area has the potential to stifle innovation. **Assist:** Develop tactics that aim to balance innovation and regulation.
Inspired value	Innovation is multiplying, inspired by the AI revolution. **Assist:** Support with appraisal tools that enable fair, transparent but strategic evaluations and ranking to key priorities. Act as mediator and co-producer when adding a strategic overlay to this burgeoning field.
Fame value	Not all fame is wanted. Fame can come from news reports on data breaches. Confidential patient data compromised. **Assist:** Accounting to support risk management practices and system audits.

4.5 Conclusion

By encompassing several contributions, the chapter serves as a foundational reference for stakeholders in the healthcare sector, aiming to understand, adopt and optimise the use of HIS in the era of VBHC.

1 **Comprehensive Analysis of the Digital Health Landscape:** The chapter offers an in-depth overview of the rising significance of digital health, predicted to value over $550 billion by 2027. It provides context to the enormous potential and need for digital health integration in the modern healthcare sector.
2 **Significance of VBHC:** The chapter elucidates the crucial role of digital technology in driving VBHC, emphasising its contribution to enhancing patient outcomes, optimising clinical decisions, and refining healthcare administration.
3 **Introduction to HIS:** A detailed definition and understanding of HIS are provided, establishing their critical function in capturing, managing and transmitting health-related information, thereby leading to improved patient care and system efficiency.
4 **Global and Regional Perspectives:** With a spotlight on Australia, the chapter analyses global efforts and investments in HIS infrastructure, offering readers insights into best practices, challenges and the tangible impacts of such systems.
5 **Differentiation between EMRs and EHRs:** The chapter informs readers on the nuances between EMRs and electronic health records (EHRs), helping them grasp the depth, scope and functionality of these systems in healthcare settings.
6 **Role of Artificial Intelligence in Healthcare:** Another contribution of this chapter is that it highlighted the transformative potential of AI in healthcare. By providing examples like predictive modelling for hospital-acquired infections, the chapter underscores AI's ability to enhance VBHC, focusing on early detection, patient monitoring and cost-effectiveness.
7 **Emphasis on Collaboration and Upskilling:** The chapter underlines the need for collaboration between technology providers and healthcare stakeholders. Additionally, it underscores the importance of workforce upskilling for optimising the use and benefits of modern HIS.

Overall, the Australian healthcare sector's future applications of digital technologies and systems should address the technology gaps and information flows to enhance communication, collaboration and overall efficiency in providing healthcare services. Integrating technology in healthcare is crucial for improving patient outcomes and administrative service delivery. Educating and training healthcare and administrative professionals to effectively and efficiently use these technologies to deliver high-quality care is equally important. Furthermore, information security and privacy-related issues should be taken into consideration when designing systems as well as when educating healthcare professionals to use those systems. Effective information flows are paramount in a VBHC model where patient outcomes and quality of care are the focus. Robust health information flow systems enable healthcare providers to make evidence-based decisions leading to better patient outcomes and reduced healthcare costs. Prioritising information flows helps with measuring value-based outcomes while monitoring the healthcare system's overall efficiency.

In conclusion, we have four key takeaways to improve HIS and information flows between different stakeholders of the industry to deliver VBHC.

Key Takeaway 1: HIS from various healthcare providers should be designed and implemented in a way to streamline the workflows between different stakeholders in the healthcare ecosystem. To do so, the systems need to have necessary integration mechanisms in place from the planning stages.

Key Takeaway 2: Privacy and security-related issues on information sharing should be addressed through appropriate governance structures, mechanisms and policies. To do so, cybersecurity oversight is required to define user roles, access levels and other procedures along and across the data flows.

Key Takeaway 3: Open IT literacy should be improved in all levels of healthcare industry stakeholders, from surgeons to general practitioners to nurses, accounting and administration staff. To do so, education and training workshops need to be organised aiming to upskill staff on IT skills, privacy, cybersecurity, ethical concerns, as well as on innovative applications (see Chapter 6 on Workforce Upskilling for Value-based Healthcare).

Key Takeaway 4: Investing in emerging technologies should be considered when innovating for the future of the healthcare industry. Recent advancements such as AI and robotics open new avenues for providing VBHC. To do so, technology providers and healthcare stakeholders need to build better relationships and work together in the long term, with accounting leading valuation and appraisal.

References

Australia's National Digital Health Strategy. (2020). Safe, seamless, and secure: Evolving health and care to meet the needs of modern Australia. Retrieved February 8, 2023, from https://www.digitalhealth.gov.au/sites/default/files/2020-11/Australia%27s%20National%20Digital%20Health%20Strategy%20-%20Safe%2C%20seamless%20and%20secure.pdf

Australian Digital Health Agency. (2019). *Secure messaging: Protecting your information*. Australian Government Department of Health and Aged Care. Retrieved March 21, 2023, from https://www.digitalhealth.gov.au/get-started-with-digital-health/secure-messaging-protecting-your-information

Australian Digital Health Agency. (2022). *Strategies and plans*. Australian Government Department of Health and Aged Care. Retrieved November 28, 2022, from https://www.digitalhealth.gov.au/about-us/strategies-and-plans

Australian Institute of Health and Welfare. (2022). *Digital health*. Australian Government Department of Health and Aged Care. Retrieved December 5, 2022, from https://www.aihw.gov.au/reports/australias-health/digital-health

Australian Private Hospitals Association. (2022). *Australian-first AI system keeps patients safe*. PH News. https://phnews.org.au/australian-first-ai-system-keeps-patients-safe/

Australian Strategic Policy Institute. (2021). *ASPI cyber maturity in the Asia-Pacific region 2021: Achieving maturity through operationalising cybersecurity*. Retrieved March 21, 2023, from https://www.aspi.org.au/report/aspi-cyber-maturity-asia-pacific-region-2021

Australian Taxation Office. (2023). *Early stage venture capital limited partnerships*. Retrieved February 17, 2023, from https://www.ato.gov.au/business/venture-capital-and-early-stage-venture-capital-limited-partnerships/early-stage-venture-capital-limited-partnerships/

Dive-Reclus, C., & Jaeger, T. M. (2022). *Digital ecosystems are the future of health care*. Harvard Business Review. Retrieved October 22, 2022, from https://hbr.org/sponsored/2022/10/digital-ecosystems-are-the-future-of-health-care

Fernández-Alemán, J. L., Señor, I. C., Lozoya, P. Á. O., & Toval, A. (2013). Security and privacy in electronic health records: A systematic literature review. *Journal of Biomedical Informatics*, *46*(3), 541–562. 10.1016/j.jbi.2012.12.003

Folio3. (2023). *Cerner vs Epic pros and cons: Which one to go for?*. https://digitalhealth.folio3.com/blog/cerner-vs-epic-pros-and-cons/

Frondelius, T., Atkova, I., Miettunen, J., Rello, J., & Jansson, M. M. (2022). Diagnostic and prognostic prediction models in ventilator-associated pneumonia: Systematic review and meta-analysis of prediction modelling studies. *Journal of Critical Care*, *67*, 44–56. 10.1016/j.jcrc.2021.10.001

Gesund Partners. (2022). *Esiselvitys toisiolain vaikutuksista sote-tietojen toisiokäyttöön tutkimus-, kehitys- ja innovaatiotoiminnassa sekä opetuksessa*. https://findata.fi/wp-content/uploads/sites/13/2022/02/Esiselvitys-toisiolain-vaikutuksista-sote-tietojen-toisiokayttoon-tutkimus-kehitys-ja-innovaatiotoiminnassa-seka-opetuksessa.pdf

Hägglund, M., McMillan, B., Whittaker, R., & Blease, C. (2022). Patient empowerment through online access to health records. *British Medical Journal*, *378*, e071531. 10.1136/bmj-2022-071531.

Healthcare Information and Management Systems Society. (2020, September 23). *Personal Health Records, Electronic Health Records, Key to India's National Digital Health Mission Comment Letter*. https://www.himss.org/resources/personal-health-records-electronic-health-records-key-indias-national-digital-health

Hendry, J. (2021). *Chamonix lands My Health Record app deal*. itnews. https://www.itnews.com.au/news/chamonix-lands-my-health-record-app-deal-572608

Jansson, M., Liisanantti, J., Ala-Kokko, T., & Reponen, J. (2022a). The negative impact of interface design, customizability, inefficiency, malfunctions, and information retrieval on user experience: A national usability survey of ICU clinical information systems in Finland. *International Journal of Medical Informatics*, *259*, 104680. 10.1016/j.ijmedinf.2021.104680

Jansson, M. M., Ohtonen, P., Alalääkkölä, T., Heikkinen, J., Mäkiniemi, M., Lahtinen, S., Lahtela, R., Ahonen, M., Jämsä, S., & Liisanantti, J. (2022b). Artificial intelligence-based technologies in surgical scheduling: Content validity assessment of required functionalities. *BMC Health Services Research*, *22*, 1513. 10.1186/s12913-022-08780-y

Jones, S., Lee, J., Hii, A., & Ko, K. (2023). Digital health in Australia: 2023. *Gilbert + Tobin*. Retrieved February 17, 2023, from https://www.gtlaw.com.au/knowledge/digital-health-australia

Kushniruk, A. (2019). The importance of health information on the internet: How it saved my life and how it can save yours. *Journal of Medical Internet Research*, *21*(10), e16690.

MBS Online. (2022). *MBS Online*. Australian Government Department of Health and Aged Care. Retrieved February 17, 2023, from http://www.mbsonline.gov.au/internet/mbsonline/publishing.nsf/Content/Home
Møller, J. K., Sørensen, M., & Hardahl, C. (2021). Prediction of risk of acquiring urinary tract infection during hospital stay based on machine-learning: A retrospective cohort study. *Plos One*, *16*(3). 10.1371/journal.pone.0248636
Mulcahy, C. (2022). What is the future of digital healthcare?. *Jabil*. https://www.jabil.com/blog/digital-health-infographic.html#:~:text=The%20digital%20health%20industry%20is,bears%20this%20out%20as%20well
Nabelsi, V., & Gagnon, S. (2017). Information technology strategy for a patient-oriented, lean, and agile integration of hospital pharmacy and medical equipment supply chains. *International Journal of Production Research*, *55*(14), 3929–3945. 10.1080/00207543.2016.1218082
O'Luanaigh, F., & Hutchison, K. (2020). *The digitalisation of Australian healthcare [White Paper]*. Equigroup Healthcare. https://www.equigroup.com/wp-content/uploads/2020/09/Digitalisation-of-Healthcare-in-Australia-Whitepaper-1.pdf
Porter, M. E., & Teisberg, E. O. (2006). *Redefining health care: Creating value-based competition on results*. Harvard Business Press.
Reis, J., Amorim, M., Melão, N., & Matos, P. (2018). *Digital transformation: A literature review and guidelines for future research [conference paper]*. Trends and Advances in Information Systems and Technologies, Naples, Italy.
Rowlands, D. (2019). *What is digital health? And why does it matter [white paper]*. Digital Health Workforce Australasia. What_is_Digital_Health.pdf (hisa.org.au).
Sicilia, M. (2022). *Oracle's acquisition of Cerner: The future of healthcare*. Cerner. Retrieved October 10, 2022, from https://www.cerner.com/perspectives/oracle-acquisition-of-cerner-the-future-of-healthcare
Snyder, K. (2023). Cerner Vs. Epic EHR (2023 Comparison). *Forbes ADVISOR*. https://www.forbes.com/advisor/business/software/cerner-vs-epic/#ease_of_use_section
Teisberg, E., Wallace, S., & O'Hara, S. (2020). Defining and implementing value-based health care: A strategic framework. *Academic Medicine*, *95*(5), 682. 10.1097/ACM.0000000000003122
The Department of Health. (2022). Information sessions running for the enhanced medical cost finder website. *AMA*. https://www.ama.com.au/ama-rounds/16-december-2022/articles/information-sessions-running-enhanced-medical-cost-finder
Tracxn. (2022). *AI in healthcare startups in Australia*. Retrieved March 1, 2023, from https://tracxn.com/explore/AI-in-Healthcare-Startups-in-Australia
Wells, L. (2022, August 18). Digital health – we have come so far, but still so much to do. *Consumers Health Forum of Australia*. https://chf.org.au/blog/digital-health-we-have-come-so-far-still-so-much-do
World Health Organization. (2021). *Global strategy on digital health 2020–2025*. World Health Organization. https://www.who.int/docs/default-source/documents/gs4dhdaa2a9f352b0445bafbc79ca799dce4d.pdf

5 Moving the Value Chain to Support Integrated Care

Vinh Thai, Shams Rahman, Gillian Vesty, Miia Jansson, Tarek Rana, Kerryn Butler-Henderson, and My Nguyen

5.1 Introduction

Achieving high operational efficiency in the healthcare sector is contingent on the implementation of supply chain management (SCM) practices (Pervez et al., 2016). This is due to the inherent challenges presented by the sector, including a large product variety, variable product life cycles, increased outsourcing, new trends in information technology (IT) and globalisation of businesses (Lee, 2002). Healthcare supply chain management (HSCM) is particularly complex, as the precision of healthcare organisations and hospitals is a matter of life and death (Mustaffa and Potter, 2009).

As discussed in the previous chapter, the COVID-19 pandemic presented an opportunity to revamp the existing fragmented health and care systems and establish integrated systems that prioritise community needs. The shift from hospital-based and disease-specific approaches towards an outcomes approach encourages a team-oriented, integrated approach which remains in flux despite the unprecedented increase in the utilisation of telehealth, eHealth and other technological support systems (Stein et al., 2020). This exemplifies the adaptability of the healthcare supply chain and of multidisciplinary teams to address the day-to-day challenges during lockdown, which was previously deemed implausible. As the COVID-19 pandemic subsides, there are calls for a new integrated healthcare model that has the potential to improve patient outcomes while optimising resource utilisation across the healthcare supply chain.

5.2 SCM in Healthcare

SCM involves the management of information, supplies and finances related to the acquisition and movement of goods and services from suppliers to end-users. It is especially critical in the healthcare industry, where errors can have life-threatening consequences (Turhan and Vayvay, 2009). There are high costs for healthcare providers and heavy dependence on third parties (Kritchanchai and Suwandechochai, 2010) with the overall aim of enhancing clinical outcomes while controlling costs (de Vries, 2011). Supply chain 'value'

DOI: 10.4324/9781032685489-5

in healthcare refers to managing the activities in the supply chain efficiently and providing optimal service for the quality and safety of patient care.

The typical hospital supply chain is a complex area with multiple flows, including physical flow, information flow and financial flow. It mobilises various resources to ensure proper functioning and customer satisfaction, especially the primary customer, the patient (Dixit et al., 2019). AI, along with the digitalisation of healthcare, has the potential to significantly enhance supply chain efficiency through time series forecasting. As one of the predictive analytics tools, it is crucial for predicting bookings and medical services and can assist in managing healthcare operations (Piccialli et al., 2021).

E-procurement uses a web interface or networked system to connect suppliers and customers. It is useful to improve supplier performance, empower suppliers with the opportunity to manage self-service, remove approval bottlenecks and increase overall efficiency and cost savings. Ultimately, the objective is to create a just-in-time (JIT) healthcare supply chain that minimises on-hand inventory but has enough to address contingencies. E-procurement supports this activity and also mitigates risks associated with invoicing and deters unethical purchasing arrangements. Importantly for the accountant, e-procurement can break down data silos and provide useful data flows for management control and performance evaluation.

Although e-procurement offers many advantages in healthcare, one of the primary obstacles is the absence of standardisation within the healthcare sector, which involves various stakeholders, such as suppliers, providers and patients, each with distinct needs and preferences. Standardising procurement procedures and systems becomes a complex task but is important for the management of costs in value-based healthcare (VBHC). Similarly, health forecasting involves predicting health situations or disease episodes in advance and can help optimise procurement for anticipated emergency department visits, daily hospital attendance and admissions (Soyiri and Reidpath, 2013).

Furthermore, **inventory control** and accuracy have been persistent challenges in the healthcare industry for many years (Rivard-Royer, 2002; Moatari-Kazerouni and Bendavid, 2017). Hospital supply chains face numerous challenges, including fragmented supplier bases, inefficiencies, excessive administrative expenses, poor management, inappropriate care and waste. Thus, effective SCM can have a positive impact on a hospital's bottom line (Balcazar-Camacho et al., 2016). Due to the constantly changing regulations and technology, as well as the unpredictability of patient mix, accurately forecasting inventories has proven to be particularly difficult for healthcare organisations. To mitigate the risks associated with poor service and patient care, hospitals typically maintain higher inventory levels compared to other industries. However, this practice often leads to inefficiencies and increased costs, without necessarily improving patient care (Rivard-Royer, 2002; Moatari-Kazerouni and Bendavid, 2017).

In addition, healthcare organisations often lack systems to monitor and control stockroom access, which can result in employees creating 'hidden stocks' to handle uncertainties in demand and avoid stock-outs (Rivard-Royer, 2002). The use of hidden stocks increases inventory holding costs and leads to inaccuracies in forecasting, as demand is driven by the intuition of doctors and nurses rather than by data. Moving to a JIT approach (Haan and Yamamoto, 1999) requires flexibility and collaboration between suppliers and users, which can result in an increase in transportation and call frequency, as well as the cost of operations. JIT may not be appropriate for life-threatening products which require a different approach. Liu et al. (2017) developed a new logistics management model for medical consumables in hospitals called 'SPD', which stands for supply, processing and distribution. The model has been studied and developed in many Japanese hospitals and has been successfully applied for over 20 years, resulting in significant reductions in logistics costs and improvements in logistics management effectiveness.

To achieve supply chain coordination, hospitals can utilise purchasing policies, inventory management and information technology such as enterprise resource planning and warehouse management systems, as well as high levels of standardisation, joint planning processes, synchronised forecasts, information sharing and aligned interests and management styles between all agents. Real-time information on inventory levels and resource availability facilitates tactical and operational planning. Coordinated supply chain planning reduces healthcare waste and enhances inventory management in healthcare (Power, 2005).

In the effort to create a more agile and responsive healthcare system, able to cope with pandemic-scale pressures, Australia has shifted its ongoing healthcare investment towards developing and implementing new technologies, with a focus on delivering value-based services (Jones et al., 2023). Telehealth, electronic prescriptions and home delivery of medications were all made possible under the Medicare Benefits Schedule during COVID-19 (MBS Online, 2022). This dramatically changed the nature of healthcare supply chains.

5.3 Digital Supply Chain and Agile Hospitals: Future Development

The adoption of HIS and information technologies in HSCM has been recognised as a key enabler to improve efficiency and effectiveness of healthcare operations. The use of radio frequency identification (RFID), bar codes and e-Kanban systems for inventory management has been proven to increase data accuracy and reduce manual errors in the healthcare supply chain (Haddara and Staaby, 2018; Pedana et al., 2017; Aguilar-Escobara et al., 2015). Moreover, technologies such as automated cart transporters, vending machines and autonomous guided vehicles (AGVs) have been found to improve material handling processes and reduce waiting times for patients (Falasca and Kros, 2018; Fragapane et al., 2018). AI and robotics have been employed in the healthcare industry to automate routine tasks, improve decision-making and reduce labour costs (Calderona et al., 2015). Additionally, emerging technologies such as additive manufacturing and 3D printing have shown great potential to revolutionise the production and customisation of medical devices and implants (Özceylan et al., 2017). Blockchain, IoT and biometrics have been proposed to improve traceability and accountability of healthcare products and services (Misra and Bisui, 2018; Shakshukia and Reid, 2015; Haddud et al., 2017). Overall, the adoption of HIS and emerging technologies in healthcare SCM offers significant opportunities to enhance supply chain performance and patient outcomes.

Various technologies have been employed at different levels in the healthcare/hospital supply chain environment, with particular focus on their potential as platforms for Lean and Agile supply chain strategies. These technologies have been found to enhance operational performance and financial benefits and are considered enablers for supply chain integration and performance management across the end-to-end supply chain, from manufacturer to patient. However, the implementation of Lean strategy in healthcare faces barriers due to a lack of established tools and limited research in this area (Costa and Filho, 2016). In the healthcare context, Lean proposes a redundancy concept in the entire supply chain, with a set of outcomes that define both the performance of the healthcare system and the development of employees and the work environment (Adebanjo et al., 2016).

Several models have been used to implement Lean in the healthcare supply chain, such as value stream mapping (Henrique et al., 2016) and Six Sigma (Wijewardana and Rupasinghe, 2016). On the other hand, agile operation is characterised by quick responsiveness, which is highly desirable in healthcare. Organisational structure, a motivated and flexible workforce, cooperation between management and employees, availability of training and the implementation of employee and patient suggestions are considered key enablers of agile performance in healthcare (Patri and Suresh, 2017).

Various methodologies have been used to measure the agility of the healthcare supply chain, such as total interpretive structural modelling (Patri and Suresh, 2017), the technique for order of preference by similarity to ideal solution (Mehralian et al., 2015), the supply chain operations reference model (Ghatari et al., 2015) and the partial least squares model (Blome et al., 2013). The combination of Lean and Agile operations, referred to as 'Leagility', is a promising approach for achieving high responsiveness in healthcare facilities while lowering the cost of the supply chain and human resources (Rahimnia and Moghadasian, 2010). Scholars have extensively studied the implementation of Lean strategy for improving hospital waste management across various fronts, including equipment control, patient scheduling, drug delivery systems, staff management and capacity planning, with a key constraint being doctors' preferences for certain products to ensure patient safety (Borges et al., 2019; Kritchanchai et al., 2018; Sloan et al., 2014). However, the generalisation of these practices across entire hospital processes remains a challenge, and this is due to obstacles such as bureaucratisation and top management commitment. Furthermore, logistics culture, patient and product flow and information flow are not sufficiently integrated into the strategic vision of hospitals (Gendy and Lahmar, 2019).

Overall, the implementation of Lean strategy for hospital waste management can yield substantial benefits, but significant challenges remain for generalising these practices across all processes. Further research is needed to identify effective strategies for overcoming the challenges of bureaucratisation and top management commitment and ensuring that logistics culture, patient and product flow and information flow are sufficiently integrated into the strategic vision of hospitals.

5.4 SCM and Integrated Care

As indicated in earlier chapters, there is growing global evidence supporting the shift from hospitals to homes for the treatment of certain conditions in an integrated way. A report conducted by EY found that in Italy, a telehealth programme for elderly patients with congestive heart failure reduced costs by 65% and lowered emergency department visits and readmissions within 30 days (McBride, 2023). Similarly, in the United States, a randomised controlled trial of acutely ill adults showed that providing care in the home reduced the adjusted mean cost of the acute episode by 38%. This was made possible through home visits, remote monitoring, virtual care, IV medication and at-home testing (McBride, 2023). Integrated care is essential to VBHC and defined as the multidisciplinary coordination of care and social services across the model of care for an individual (Royal Australasian College of Physicians, 2018). Integrated care involves the provision of seamless, effective and efficient care that reflects the whole of a person's health needs:

- From prevention through to end of life.
- Across both physical, psychosocial and mental health.
- In partnership with the individual, carers and family members.

Integrated care has a significant impact on hospital SCM and resource allocation, which in turn can impact multiple stakeholders within the system, including the role of the accountant. As mentioned in Chapter 4, there are more technologies that are now cloud-based which creates a significant impact on the profit and loss (P&L) statement and as a result there is more room for capital but also an opportunity for procurement.

In 2016, the WHO classified integrated care models based on the extent to which integration occurs, ranging from individuals with chronic conditions and disease-specific models through to population-based integrated models.

Of interest for this study are the individual and group approaches to focusing on how to achieve VBHC outcomes through individualised integrated care or grouping patients according to their chronic or disease conditions.

- **Individual models of integrated care:** This category of integrated care models focuses on the coordination of care for high-risk patients and/or those with multiple conditions and their caregivers. Individual models of integrated care strive to facilitate the proper delivery of healthcare services and overcome fragmentation among providers (Bodenheimer, 2008), aiming for integration across the patient's entire lifespan rather than just one episode of care. The design and integration processes underlying individual models described in the literature can vary. Some of the well-known models include case management, individual care plans, patient-centred medical home and personal health budgets.
- **Group- and disease-specific models:** Chronic care model, integrated care models for elderly and frail, and disease-specific integrated care models.

A key goal of VBHC and integrated care is vertical integration (Curry and Ham, 2010) which brings together organisations at different levels of the hierarchical structure under one management umbrella by integrating primary and secondary care, or general practice and community care. Virtual integration is about the formation of alliances, networks and contractual arrangements. The different perspectives shaping integrated care are highlighted in Figure 5.1.

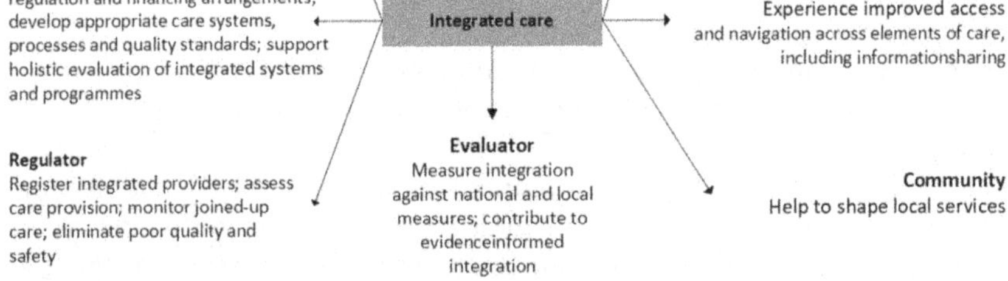

Source: World Health Organization, 2016.

Figure 5.1 Perspectives Shaping Integrated Care.

Note: Adapted from *Integrated care models: An overview* by World Health Organization, 2016 (https://www.euro.who.int/__data/assets/pdf_file/0005/322475/Integrated-care-models-overview.pdf). Copyright © 2016 by The Regional Office for Europe of the World Health Organization.

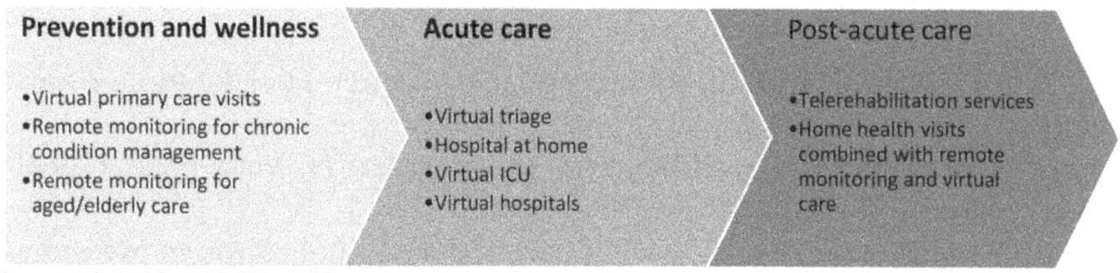

Source: Adapted from McBride, 2023.

Figure 5.2 Hybrid Care Models Using Virtual Care and Remote Monitoring Across the Care Spectrum.

Note: Adapted from *How virtual and merge for a healthier and more sustainable future health systems* by McBride, A., 2023 (https://www.ey.com/en_au/health/how-virtual-and-in-person-care-merge-for-a-healthier-and-more-sustainable-future). Copyright © 2023 by EY.

An important and emerging aspect of integrated care is the **hybrid care delivery models**. That is, models of care that rely on a combination of telehealth and in-person care. In leveraging connected digital platforms, these systems of care are proactive and data-driven and designed to help patients remain healthy and at home for longer periods. Figure 5.2 highlights the varying degrees of coordinated and integrated hybrid care.

The use of hybrid delivery models by hospitals is described as Hospital in the Home (HITH) but can also be set up for primary care to avoid hospital admission. Whether for primary care or post-surgery, care teams assist patients in setting up wearables and other connected devices that enable the monitoring of vital biometric data remotely, by clinicians who are located at a centralised digital command centre. System alerts may prompt a virtual call or home visit. To fully support the integration of telehealth and in-office appointments, healthcare providers must establish comprehensive and interconnected patient workflows that encompass various touchpoints. Virtual appointments are just one aspect of this process. The workflows, such as appointment scheduling, digital patient registration, automated appointment reminders, two-way patient text communication and follow-up after care, are crucial in this regard. Once data flows are in place, the use of AI can support predictive analytics for individuals and contribute with insights for overall population health (Smith and Al-Razouki, 2019).

Across Australia there are state- and territory-wide strategies that coordinate and encourage better communication and connectivity between healthcare providers supported by technological enablers. Important principle in the integrated care approach is the collective accountability with all service providers sharing responsibility for the person's well-being. The information flows between sectors, organisations, teams and clinicians, with a single record gathered from a shared assessment, that helps to link data to identify and analyse patient care pathways (Tzimos, 2020). Planning and monitoring capacity is in place.

The benefits of taking an integrated care approach are that:

- Patients, families and carers experiencing better coordination of care across different settings.
- Improved health and well-being of the population, with greater health literacy and self-care.
- A more value-based health system with reduced duplication in investment and services and more effective use of resources.
- Greater job satisfaction for service providers, clinicians and other staff, with improved experiences of providing care (https://www.health.nsw.gov.au/integratedcare/).

Phased plans drawing on digital health technologies are in place to establish joint governance between key stakeholders in the primary health networks and hospitals so that future services can be designed and delivered to support specific patient groupings with common disease conditions.

At the federal level, one interviewee discussed the importance of a centralised purchasing mechanism for Australian hospitals, electronic monitoring of stock for tracking and supplier management, along with the need for standardised treatment pathways, for streamlined inventory procurement. Statistics on usage by the different hospital networks in comparison to activity can provide useful benchmarks for performance measurement, audit and reporting. The interviewee provided an outline of the procurement reform that is currently underway at the federal level. *The intent is to ultimately remove the need of the frontline staff to spend time in storerooms … to monitor remotely … We ultimately want to get to the point where there is sufficient data to tell us when we need to ship things straight into the ward, not even to the dock.* As a result, there is a huge investment in resources to reorganise the storerooms as well as ensure that everything is counted and checked off remotely to track and trace everything through the hospitals.

However, with care becoming integrated and hybrid, the notion of the storeroom is also changing. The HITH environment is managed according to federal and state ABF funding provisions. Individual technologically connected monitoring initiatives, such as blood glucose monitoring, and AI predictive analytics on past care, are available but depend on the network provider and degree of experimentation with initiatives to keep patients out of hospital. Bundled care arrangements and technological innovations are still in their infancy, with revolutionary impacts to the supply chain delivery, still to come.

One interviewee explained that particularly during the height of the COVID-19 pandemic they had to profile remote care and virtual emergency initiatives without proper funding classifications. This was where hospitals interfaced with the GPs, but this created other problems such as the potential for double counting (i.e., through Medicare patients for GP visits as well as ABF funding the hospital for care). As a result, the interviewee believed this has stymied what is a suitable and sustainable way forward in terms of a classification. Whereas, with HITH, it is the approach that is more popular because it does have a classification and activity that attracts ABF funding. *So, it's easy to scale from HITH and you can see the case is pretty straightforward.* The interviewee further explained that there is a value chain way to think about the activity offerings and the need to move barriers and disincentives and that, *most of the time we end up, you know, fixing something by breaking something else.*

Currently, with HITH, healthcare workers visit patients in their home and bring the supplies with them from the hospital. These include equipment, disposables, dressings and drugs dispensed from pharmacy. The vehicles are owned by the hospital and the clinicians travel to the vehicle depot, which is based at the base hospital, or at one of its satellite sites, such as smaller hospitals that belong to the same network. They work to a roster and visit patients in their home for the prescribed care. Electronic records will travel with the clinician who can update care delivery and test results remotely, for other medical team or specialists to review in real-time through connected mobile apps.

Interestingly, at one large teaching hospital, the HITH team was explaining that they plan to upgrade their vehicles to an electric fleet but had trouble with the vehicle boot space. As can be imagined, there needs to be capacity for refrigerated medication, or secured medication containment, along with enough space for mobile equipment and a range of disposables. The HITH car becomes a remote storeroom of inventory that needs to be managed and circulated to ensure use-by dates have not expired. As explained in the interviews, electronic tagging through RFID, bar codes and e-Kanban systems can support this mobile storeroom. However, at the next level of procurement, the head of the department explained that sustainability is extremely important to them, and the move to electric vehicles is essential and capacity management will have to work. This provides an interesting case study for accounting to consider how to incorporate sustainability impacts into investment appraisal/leasing arrangements. A follow-up on how the decision was made will be interesting to note.

While the expansion of home-based care is exciting and a positive contribution to VBHC and the quadruple aim, a key point was raised by several hospital service providers. Despite the rapidly changing environment and expanding service capacity, some patients cannot be visited in the home. It is either too dangerous for the clinician – i.e., patients or family members are aggressive and there is potential for violence, or the home itself is deemed unsafe or inaccessible. Some clinicians might do home visits with a support staff, or the patients will have to come to hospital for outpatient care or be discharged to the care of the GP. This circles back to the issue of standardised care pathways and streamlined procurement. There will always be outliers to manage.

Another example of procurement activities that impact accounting is with selection of vendors. Standardising supplies means that ordering cannot be done to meet individual clinician preference for one vendor's products over another. A choice must be determined to meet standard pathways of care. Sometimes vendors promote new products. An example provided was with prosthetics (artificial joints) whereby vendors will claim that a new prosthetic that is more expensive (e.g., a knee replacement that is $28,000 instead of $15,000) but might reduce the patient length of stay. It comes down to the evidence and whether there will be a reduction in patient stay, as this creates an opportunity for freeing up the bed early. The role for accounting is to support the business case for change.

Box 5.1 Insights from Finland

As indicated in Chapter 2, *the move to VBHC in Finland has resulted in restructuring of budgets. Now local networks are provided block funds, determined by local needs (i.e., general health of patients and longitudinal use of health resources across primary care, social services and hospital care). The incentive is now to avoid costly hospital treatments with a focus on preventative health. As a result of a shift in budgeting there will be a shift in resource allocation. This gives rise to a more nuanced understanding of the costs of quality in healthcare, with more resourcing being provided in upstream preventative care to eliminate downstream failure costs, which are measured in terms of poor patient outcomes. Given this is a relatively new undertaking, it will provide an interesting study to assess the changes to resourcing overtime, from both workforce as well as the medical supplies, medicines and other inventory assets.*

5.5 Strategy Implications for Supply/Value Chain Management

Given the advances in technology in e-procurement and inventory management, along with the efficiencies associated with centralised procurement, there is a need for accounting to help identify and support opportunities for standardisation across the value chain as well as identifying waste and non-value-added activities. Opportunities for performance evaluation and benchmarking from supply chain and logistics management activities can help identify the success of moving towards distributed and hybrid care arrangements which are all part of integrated VBHC. In Table 5.1, the strategic approaches and underlying values that shape this sector are identified as part of building a framework for VBHC implementation.

Table 5.1 A strategic values-based framework for VBHC implementation

Strategy/Values	*How can accountants support?*
Expand partnerships	Detail the emerging **value/supply chain management** system where the population benefits from **distributed hybrid care** arrangements, such as HITH. Supply chain management for **integrated care** is essential in the move to VBHC. **Assist:** Build co-producer activities between clinicians, accountants, supply chain and logistics managers to support performance evaluation and streamline integrated care activities.
Industrial value	The focus on costs and efficiency is evident in the technology advances supporting healthcare supply chain and logistics. Work to manage standardisation of operational stock keeping units for efficient procurement as well as standardisation of data flows supports overall efficiency and secure systems. **Assist:** Industrial value is important in this sector. As hospital boundaries change and potential restructuring as part of VBHC takes place, work to standardise data flows for efficient and secure outcomes.
Market value	The market is competitive with suppliers and potential suppliers with new innovative healthcare solutions. Compromise is managed with centralised government-management procurement. There are complexities that need to be considered, such as remote access and delivery of care to patients in their homes. **Assist:** Support with standardisation with evaluation and ranking of suppliers that meet strategic priorities. Ensure logistics management that enables fair and equitable access. Use cost of quality principles to determine best use of resourcing across the value chain.
Domestic value	The centralised procurement processes provide a hierarchy to support standardisation. However, local needs have competing priorities that call on support to manage the different value perspectives. **Assist:** Support with standardisation techniques and tools of evaluation that critique alternate strategies.
Civic value	Regulatory oversight of advanced e-procurement provides the opportunity for streamlined practices and capacity to deliver as hospital walls dissipate. **Assist:** Develop compliance practices and performance data for benchmarking.
Inspired value	Innovation is multiplying and inspired by the AI revolution and the move to preventative health. **Assist:** Support with appraisal tools that foster a shift in resource demands and costs of quality appraisal across the entire health value-chain.

(*Continued*)

Table 5.1 (Continued)

Strategy/Values	*How can accountants support?*
Fame value	As with HIS, not all fame is wanted. Fame can come from news reports on data breaches. Logistics and supply chain management issues can impact delivery of care, through poor quality products, or supply issues. The COVID-19 pandemic revealed the challenges of supply, such as personal, protective, equipment (PPE), lack of ventilator and intensive care beds as well as staff shortages. **Assist:** Accounting to support risk modelling and risk management practices.

5.6 Conclusion

In summary, this chapter offers a few contributions to support the ongoing transformations within the healthcare sector, emphasising the role of technology, strategic approaches and integrated models in reshaping the future of healthcare delivery and its SCM.

1 **Holistic Evaluation of HSCM Evolution:** The chapter provides an in-depth analysis of the HSCM and its importance in modern healthcare, especially given the intricacies it presents in pandemic situations like COVID-19.
2 **Redefining Health Systems Post-Pandemic:** This chapter underscores the COVID-19 pandemic's role as a catalyst for healthcare transformation, encouraging a shift from fragmented systems to more comprehensive, integrated models that serve community's healthcare needs better.
3 **Technological Advancements in HSCM:** The chapter delves into a detailed examination of various technological integrations, from eHealth to AI, that have fortified the healthcare supply chain's efficiency and adaptability.
4 **Synergy between Technology and Lean/Agile Strategies:** By emphasising the convergence of healthcare technologies with 'Lean and Agile' supply chain strategies, the chapter showcases the potential to boost operational performance and deliver optimal patient outcomes.
5 **Global Paradigm Shift in Healthcare Delivery:** Drawing on global evidence, the chapter elaborates on the transition from hospital-centric models to home-based treatments. It highlights successful telehealth programmes and other integrated care strategies that not only reduce costs but also enhance patient well-being.
6 **Deep Dive into Integrated Care:** The chapter offers a profound understanding of integrated care, essential to VBHC. It elaborates on its significance in coordinating multidisciplinary healthcare services across different care phases and its far-reaching impact on HSCM and various stakeholders.

7 **Exploration of WHO's Integrated Care Models:** The chapter provides readers with a comprehensive breakdown of the WHO's classification of integrated care models. This includes an in-depth look into both individual-centric and group-specific models, providing insights into their design, integration processes, and objectives.
8 **Highlighting the Aim of VBHC and Integrated Care:** Concluding with a focus on the future of healthcare, the chapter sheds light on the goal of achieving 'vertical and virtual integration'. This aims to bring together varied healthcare service providers under unified management or through strategic alliances, charting the path forward for the global healthcare industry.

In conclusion, we have three key takeaways for greater understanding of the impacts of VBHC on supply chain and logistics management. With the move towards preventative care, and potential change in budgeting and performance/reward implications, there is opportunity for a change in measurement of the costs of quality across the healthcare value chain. By focusing on measuring patient outcomes, as a proxy for quality cost measurement this will shift resourcing along the healthcare value chain.

Key Takeaway 1: From a supply chain and logistics management perspective, virtual care and in-person care needs to be balanced and managed. There are multiple factors that impact standardisation of delivery which impact on value-chain costs.

Key Takeaway 2: Accounting can support with insights to the impacts of changes in budgeting across the healthcare value chain to resourcing and procurement.

Key Takeaway 3: Accounting can support with enhanced cost of quality measures across the healthcare value chain by linking patient outcome measures to resourcing and procurement.

References

Adebanjo, D., Laosirihongthong, T., & Samaranayake, P. (2016). Prioritizing lean supply chain management initiatives in healthcare service operations: A fuzzy AHP approach. *Production Planning and Control*, *27*(12), 953–966. 10.1080/09537287.2016.1164909

Aguilar-Escobara, V. G., Bourque, S., & Godino-Gallego, N. (2015). Hospital Kanban system implementation: Evaluating satisfaction of nursing personnel. *Investigaciones Europeas de Dirección y Economía de la Empresa*, *21*(3), 101–110. 10.1016/j.iedee.2014.12.001

Balcazar-Camacho, D. A., Lopez-Bello, C. A., & Adarme-Jaimes, W. (2016). Strategic guidelines for supply chain coordination in healthcare and a mathematical model as a proposed mechanism for the measurement of coordination effects. *DYNA*, *83*(197), 203–211. 10.15446/dyna.v83n197.55596

Blome, D., Schoenherr, T., & Rexhausen, C. (2013). Antecedents and enablers of supply chain agility and its effect on performance: A dynamic capabilities perspective. *International Journal of Production Research*, *51*(4), 1295–1318. 10.1080/00207543.2012.728011

Bodenheimer, T. (2008). Coordinating care – A perilous journey through the health care system. *New England Journal of Medicine*, *358*(10), 1064.

Borges, G. A., Tortorella, G., Rossini, M., & Portioli-Staudacher, A. (2019). Lean implementation in health care supply chain: A scoping review. *Journal of Health Organization and Management*, *33*(3), 304–322. 10.1108/JHOM-06-2018-0176

Calderona, C. A. A., Mohan, E. R., & Ng, B. S. (2015). Development of a hospital mobile platform for logistics tasks. *Digital Communications and Networks*, *1*(2), 102–111. 10.1016/j.dcan.2015.03.001

Costa, L. B. M., & Filho, M. G. (2016). Lean healthcare: Review, classification and analysis of literature. *Production Planning and Control*, *27*(10), 823–836. 10.1080/09537287.2016.1143131

Curry, N., & Ham, C. (2010). *Clinical and service integration: The route to improved outcomes*. The King's Fund. https://www.kingsfund.org.uk/sites/default/files/Clinical-and-service-integration-Natasha-Curry-Chris-Ham-22-November-2010.pdf

de Vries, J. (2011). The shaping of inventory systems in health services: A stakeholder analysis. *International Journal of Production Economics*, *133*(1), 60–69. 10.1016/j.ijpe.2009.10.029

Dixit, A., Routroy, S., & Dubey, S. K. (2019). A systematic literature review of healthcare supply chain and implications of future research. *International Journal of Pharmaceutical and Healthcare Marketing*, *13*(4), 405–435. 10.1108/IJPHM-05-2018-0028

Falasca, M., & Kros, J. F. (2018). Success factors and performance outcomes of healthcare industrial vending systems: An empirical analysis. *Technological Forecasting and Social Change*, *126*, 41–52. 10.1016/j.techfore.2016.06.024

Fragapane, G. I., Bertnum, A. B., Hvolby, H., & Strandhagen, J. O. (2018). Materials distribution and transportation in Norwegian hospital: A case study. *International Journal of Automatic Control*, *51*(11), 352–357. 10.1016/j.ifacol.2018.08.316

Gendy, A. W. Al, & Lahmar, A. (2019). 'Review on healthcare supply chain', Proceedings of IEEE/ACS International Conference on Computer Systems and Applications, AICCSA. IEEE, 2019-Novem. doi: 10.1109/AICCSA47632.2019.9035234

Ghatari, A. R., Mehralian, G., Zarenezhad, F., & Rasekh, H. (2015). Developing a model for agile supply: An empirical study from Iranian pharmaceutical supply chain. *International Journal of Pharmaceutical and Healthcare Marketing*, *9*, 189–201.

Haan, J. de, & Yamamoto, M. (1999). Zero inventory management: Facts or fiction? Lessons from Japan. *International Journal of Production Economics*, *59*(1), 65–75. 10.1016/S0925-5273(98)00022-X

Haddara, M., & Staaby, A. (2018). RFID applications and adoptions in healthcare: A review on patient safety. *Procedia Computer Science*, *138*, 80–88. 10.1016/j.procs.2018.10.012

Haddud, A., DeSouza, A., Khare, A., & Lee, H. (2017). Examining potential benefits and challenges associated with the Internet of Things integration in supply chains. *Journal of Manufacturing Technology Management*, *28*(8), 1055–1085. 10.1108/JMTM-05-2017-0094

Henrique, D. B., Rentes, A. F., Godinho Filho, M., & Esposto, K. F. (2016). A new value stream mapping approach for healthcare environments. *Production Planning and Control*, 27(1), 24–48. 10.1080/09537287.2015.1051159

Jones, S., Lee, J., Hii, A., & Ko, K. (2023). Digital health in Australia: 2023. *Gilbert + Tobin*. Retrieved February 17, 2023, from https://www.gtlaw.com.au/knowledge/digital-health-australia

Kritchanchai, D., & Suwandechochai, R. (2010). Supply chain management in health sector in Thailand: A case study. *International Journal of Services, Economics and Management*, 2(2), 211–224. 10.1504/IJSEM.2010.03092

Kritchanchai, D., Engelseth, P., & Srisakunwan, S. (2018, December 16–19). *Implementing and using new information technology in hospital logistics [Conference session]*. International Conference on Industrial Engineering and Engineering Management, Bangkok, Thailand. 10.1109/IEEM.2018.8607418

Lee, H. L. (2002). Aligning supply chain strategies with product uncertainties. *California Management Review*, *44*(3), 105–119. Retrieved from https://journals.sagepub.com/doi/pdf/10.2307/41166135

Liu, T., Shen, A., Hu, X., Tong, G., & Gu, W. (2017). The application of collaborative business intelligence technology in the hospital SPD logistics management model. *Iranian Journal of Public Health*, *46*(6), 744–754.

MBS Online. (2022). *MBS Online*. Australian Government Department of Health and Aged Care. Retrieved February 17, 2023, from http://www.mbsonline.gov.au/internet/mbsonline/publishing.nsf/Content/Home

McBride, A. (2023). *How virtual and merge for a healthier and more sustainable future Health systems*. EY. https://www.ey.com/en_au/health/how-virtual-and-in-person-care-merge-for-a-healthier-and-more-sustainable-future

Mehralian, G., Moosivand, A., Emadi, S., & Asgharian, R. (2015). Developing a coordination framework for pharmaceutical supply chain: using analytical hierarchy process. *International Journal of Logistics Systems and Management*, *26*(3), 277–293. 10.1504/IJLSM.2017.10002596

Misra, S. C., & Bisui, S. (2018). Modelling vital success factors in adopting personalized medicine system in healthcare technology and management. *Engineering Science and Technology*, *21*(3), 532–545. 10.1016/j.jestch.2018.04.011

Moatari-Kazerouni, A., & Bendavid, Y. (2017). Improving logistics processes of surgical Instruments. *Business Process Management Journal*, *23*(2), 448–466. 10.1108/BPMJ-06-2016-0127

Mustaffa, N. H., & Potter, A. (2009). Healthcare supply chain management in Malaysia: A case study. *Supply Chain Management*, *14*(3), 234–243. 10.1108/13598540910954575

Özceylan, E., Çetinkaya, C., Demirel, N., & Sabırlıoğlu, O. (2017). Impacts of additive manufacturing on supply chain flow: A simulation approach in healthcare industry. *Logistics*, *2*(1), 1. 10.3390/logistics2010001

Patri, R., & Suresh, M. (2017). Modelling the enablers of agile performance in healthcare organization: A TISM approach. *Global Journal of Flexible Systems Management*, *18*(3), 251–272. 10.1007/s40171-017-0160-x

Pedana, M., Gregor, M., & Plinta, D. (2017) Implementation of automated guided vehicle system in healthcare facility. *Procedia Engineering*, *192*, 665–670. 10.1016/j.proeng.2017.06.115

Pervez, M. N., Mahmud, J., & Bachar, S. C. (2016). Supply chain management of pharmaceutical products in hospitals: A case study in a privately owned tertiary level hospital. *Quest Journals Journal of Research in Business and Management*, *4*, 14–23. ISSN: 2347–3002. https://www.questjournals.org/jrbm/papers/vol4-issue4/C441423.pdf

Piccialli, F., Giampaolo F., Prezioso, E., Camacho D., & Acampora G., (2021). Artificial intelligence and healthcare: Forecasting of medical bookings through multi-source time-series fusion. *Information Fusion*, *74*, 1–16. doi: 10.1016/j.inffus.2021.03.004

Power, D. (2005). Supply chain management integration and implementation: A literature review. *Supply Chain Management*, *10*(4), 252–263. 10.1108/13598540510612721

Rahimnia, F., & Moghadasian, M. (2010). Supply chain legality in professional services: How to apply decoupling point concept in healthcare delivery system. *Supply Chain Management*, *15*(1), 80–91. 10.1108/13598541011018148

Rivard-Royer, H. (2002). Hybrid stockless: A case study: Lessons for healthcare supply chain integration. *International Journal of Operations & Production Management*, *22*(4), 412–424. 10.1108/01443570210420412

Royal Australasian College of Physicians. (2018). *Integrated care: Physicians supporting better patient outcomes [Discussion paper]*. Retrieved April 13, 2023, from https://www.racp.edu.au/docs/default-source/advocacy-library/integrated-care-physicians-supporting-better-patient-outcomes-discussion-paper.pdf

Shakshukia, E., & Reid, M. (2015). Multi-agent system applications in healthcare: Current technology and future roadmap. *Procedia Computer Science*, *52*, 252–261. 10.1016/j.procs.2015.05.071

Sloan, T., Fitzgerald, A., Hayes, K., Radnor, Z., Robinson, S., & Sohal, S. (2014). Lean in healthcare – History and recent developments. *Journal of Health Organization and Management*, *28*(2), 130–134. 10.1108/JHOM-04-2014-0064

Smith, S., & Al-Razouki, M. (2019) Hybrid healthcare. *Journal of Nursing and Patient Health Care*, *1*(1), 105. doi: 10.15744/2767-9292.1.105

Soyiri, I. N., & Reidpath, D. D. (2013). An overview of health forecasting. *Environmental Health and Preventive Medicine*, *18*(1), 1–9. 10.1007/s12199-012-0294-6

Stein, V. K., Goodwin, N., & Miller, R. (2020). From crisis to coordination: Challenges and opportunities for integrated care posed by the COVID-19 pandemic. *International Journal of Integrated Care*, *20*(3), 1–3. 10.5334/ijic.5595

Turhan, S. N., & Vayvay, O. (2009). Modeling of VMI implementation via SOA in a healthcare supply chain. *Proceedings of the 6th European and Mediterranean Conference on Information Systems, Izmir, Turkey*, 1–11.

Tzimos, A. (2020). Victorian integrated care model, supporting better integration of care between primary care and hospital services. *International Journal of Integrated Care*, *20*(S1), 1–8. 10.5334/ijic.s4170

Wijewardana, A. R. L., & Rupasinghe, T. D. (2016). Lean healthcare framework for Sri Lankan healthcare supply chains: A case study of teaching hospitals. *Universal Journal of Management*, *4*(10), 517–527. 10.13189/ujm.2016.041001

World Health Organization. (2016). *Integrated care models: An overview*. The Regional Office for Europe of the World Health Organization. https://www.euro.who.int/__data/assets/pdf_file/0005/322475/Integrated-care-models-overview.pdf

6 Workforce Upskilling for Value-Based Healthcare

Gillian Vesty, Miia Jansson, Tarek Rana, Kerryn Butler-Henderson, and Salma Arabi

6.1 Introduction

As indicated throughout this book, there is a significant change occurring in the healthcare sector. This book focused on the move towards value-based healthcare (VBHC), under varying guises of meeting the quadruple aim, a value-based approach to measure, deliver and pay. Digital health interventions are key to this change initiative that aims to focus on measuring and paying for health outcomes. Digital health technologies have the potential to improve care transitions, in terms of providing highly sophisticated systems for capturing and measuring data for performance measurement as well as extending to artificial intelligence (AI) for predictive modelling. However, health information technologies can also exacerbate existing health disparities (Vollbrecht et al., 2020), particularly where technology is not available, is one-sided (i.e., where the provider has capacity but the receiver does not, or vice versa) and if understanding is limited.

As such, there is a great need to strengthen digital health literacy in society to improve patient engagement, empowerment and outcomes (Busse et al., 2022), as well as healthcare provider capabilities. There is a need to train and improve healthcare providers on their digital health competency so that they can counsel and guide patients (Jarva et al., 2022b) as well as train administrators, which includes accountants on providing transparent data for improved decision-making and ultimately health outcomes. From an accounting perspective, it is essential that accountants are upskilled to ensure they have the capacity to meet their professional ethical obligations and act in the best interest of society (http://www.ifac.org).

In recent years, the relationship between patients, healthcare professionals and administrators has changed significantly due to digitalisation. Healthcare providers (clinicians and administrators) need to work together to become co-producers in using digital health technologies, especially given that the healthcare recipients – i.e., the patients – are increasingly becoming agents in their own care. However, these health information systems and patient engagement technologies can only be broadly effective if all healthcare stakeholders are able to access, use and effectively understand them (Vollbrecht et al., 2020).

DOI: 10.4324/9781032685489-6

6.2 Hybridised Skills Requirements

The changing role of healthcare providers and expected future skills is becoming increasingly evident with the rapid technology-based transformation. This has in some respects supported the move to VBHC, through enhanced opportunities to measure healthcare service delivery outcomes. This includes patient-reported outcome measures (PROs) as well as aligned resources to maximise VBHC outcomes across the entire value chain. Healthcare providers need strong professional knowledge and skills to integrate digital health technologies into administrative and clinical practice to provide high-quality and ethical care. Providers also need training to use PRO data for shared decision-making and population health management (Hsiao et al., 2019).

The clinical-directed skills outlined in this chapter are relevant for accountants and other healthcare administrators to effectively discharge their responsibilities and accountabilities. From an accounting perspective, this links with the requirements of the International Ethical Standards Board for Accountants (IESBA), Code of Ethics for Professional Accountants (the Code) which flows into Australian professional guidelines. The first section of the Code (Section 100) explicitly states: "A distinguishing mark of the accountancy profession is its acceptance of the responsibility to act in the public interest. A Professional Accountant's responsibility is not exclusively to satisfy the needs of an individual client or employing organisation. Therefore, the Code contains requirements and application material to enable Professional Accountants to meet their responsibility to act in the public interest" (International Ethical Standards Board for Accountants [IESBA], 2022).

The **principles** outlined in the Code to help professional accountants comply with the obligation of acting in the public interest, establish the expected standards of behaviour and include:

- Integrity
- Objectivity
- Professional competence and due care
- Confidentiality
- Professional behaviour

Thus, professional accountants are expected to provide informed expert advice and guidance, including professional duty such as compliance with mandatory technical requirements to respond to a formal investigation by the professional association (see Figure 6.1).

Because of the complex technical environments in which professional accountants find themselves operating, like healthcare institutions, the technical requirements of the role are becoming increasingly challenging, especially with the advancements in AI and data analytics. It is essential to understand the algorithms in the data and the potential biases that may well be hidden.

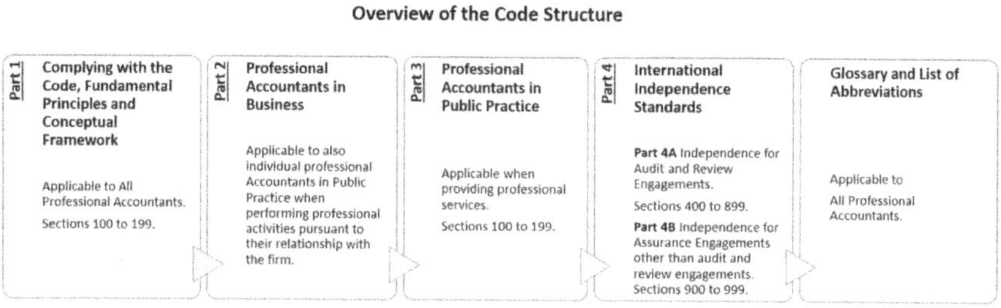

Figure 6.1 Overview of the Code of Ethics for Professional Accountants (the Code).

Note: Adapted from "Handbook of the International Code of Ethics for Professional Accountants, including International Independence Standards (2022 digital ed.)" by International Ethics Standards Board for Accountants, 2022 (https://www.ethicsboard.org/). Copyright © 2022 by International Federation Accountants.

In connecting with clinicians' view of digital health competency, which refers to healthcare providers' knowledge, skills and attitudes (Table 6.1), accountants can provide a more holistic understanding of competencies required for this sector. Digital health competencies aim to provide knowledge, skills and attitudes to delivering patient-centric care through digital channels, using digital technologies and health systems, interacting with patient through digital means, evaluating what digital health entails, combining digital approaches with traditional methods and evaluating professional competence (Jarva et al., 2022b). While accountants do not need detailed understanding of the clinical skills, outlined in Table 6.1, they do need to understand the data flows, cost, investment and performance requirements that contribute to improved outcomes in service delivery. They need to understand some of the key (and somewhat powerful) stakeholders who oversee the clinical directorates and demand prioritised resource allocation.

It is also important to recognise that diverse personal attributes (e.g., willingness, ability, confidence, self-resilience, motivation, change resistance and fears) as well as psychosocial and organisational factors (e.g., job position, changing healthcare practices, collegial, managerial and technical support) are known to affect digital health competencies (Jarva et al., 2022b; Konttila et al., 2019) and willingness to invest in upskilling. Achieving appropriate digital health competence requires regular evaluation, training and support when using new technologies (Jarva et al., 2022a; Konttila et al., 2019). Auditing practices and monitoring are operative ways to provide individual support (Konttila et al., 2019). In addition to digital health competencies, it is argued that healthcare providers need AI-related clinical competencies (https://healthitanalytics.com/news/researchers-outline-ai-related-clinical-competencies-for-health-professionals. As evidenced in earlier chapters of this book, AI is an increasingly important research focus for clinicians and is essential that accountants **support AI research** in this field with performance measurement and cost-benefit analysis of outcomes of the

Table 6.1 Important competences for future healthcare providers

Category of skills	*Subcategories of skills*	*Description*
Ethical skills	Ethical skills	• Ability to assess how to provide equal services. • Ability to recognise ethical issues in the use of digital technology in patient care (e.g., ethics, legal and regulations). • Knowledge of data privacy and security.
Digital skills	Basic digital skills	• Competence to use information technology and digital health systems. • Health information and media literacy. • Competence to design digital health systems.
	Advanced digital skills	• Digital skills to provide high-quality care. • Ability to solve practical problems in technology use. • Knowledge of digital health and its possibilities.
	Data skills	• Data management skills. • Documentation competency.
Clinical skills	Clinical knowledge	• Knowledge of clinical practices and procedures. • Knowledge of pharmacology. • Knowledge of nursing service systems. • Analytical skills.
	Professional skills	• Social interaction skills to communicate with different stakeholders and patients' relatives. • Practical skills. • Triaging skills.
Soft skills	Patient-centric care	• Ability to acknowledge the patient's willingness to use digital health services. • Ability to evaluate the patients' digital capabilities. • Ability to incorporate patient's needs into digital health services. • Ability to give responsibility to patients and set goals together with them.
	Communication skills	• Counsel patients in digital environments. • Competence in communication. • Interaction skills. • Competence in writing.
	Decision-making skills	• Ability to make autonomous and intuitive decisions.

Table 6.2 Skillset for AI-related clinical competencies

Category of skills	*Subcategories of skills*	*Description*
Digital skills	Basic AI knowledge	• Ability to explain what AI is. • Ability to describe healthcare applications from both clinical and administrative perspectives.
	Data mining	• Ability to integrate diverse information sources to create patient-centric care plans. • Ability to integrate diverse information sources to generate cost and performance measurement data.
	Advanced AI skills	• Ability to evaluate the quality, accuracy, safety, contextual appropriateness and biases of AI-based tools and their underlying data sets.
Ethical skills	Ethics of AI	• Ability to explain how social, economic and political systems influence AI-based tools and how these relationships impact justice, equity and ethics (including accounting ethics).

Note:
Adapted from "Competencies for the use of artificial intelligence–based tools by health care professionals" by Russell, R. G., Novak, L. L., Patel, M., Garvey, K. V., Craig, K. J. T., Jackson, G. P., Moore, D., & Miller, B. M., 2022, *Academic Medicine, 98*(3), 348–356 (https://doi.org/10.1097/ACM.0000000000004963). Copyright © 2022 by the *Journal of the Association of American Medical Colleges.*

proposed AI environment. It is also crucial to support in risk management of any proposed or newly introduced AI or other digital health solutions (Russell et al., 2022). This additional skillset is outlined in Table 6.2.

6.3 Strategic Support Service Provision: Changing Role of Accounting

From the interviews undertaken in this study, it has been recognised that most of the work being performed by accountants in a healthcare setting has revolved around data entry and as one interviewee, a senior accountant, said, *are transaction oriented.* This interviewee considered it was an outcome of Australian education, making them very linear and too exacting on results. Little has been done in understanding what the data means, and what the economic factors are that impact the hospital they are working in. They need more **analytic skills** in order to: *Look beyond the numbers … . have relationships, talk to people, not just behind the desk and look at the numbers as it's everything. Sometimes we spot the errors too late.* They need, *relationships and non-financial data.* Another interviewee explained that accounting *value analyses so far is retrospective, so we don't have yet, the ability to* *prospectively, use that in a budgetary sense.* This interviewee raised the importance of developing **negotiation skills** around where the value is and who should get the benefit. *We are grappling with disinvestment reinvestment.* The interviewee claimed that accountants need to know where the budgetary pressures are and why they are not **meeting value outcomes** but: *that will change once we get more data. [stop investing in] things that we shouldn't be doing and reinvest that in what's important ... that's a negotiation. So, if anything it's about negotiation skills for accountants.*

Another interviewee mentioned that negotiation was about determining whether the data was robust enough to be counted and costed and used in performance appraisal. This interviewee explained that the hospital *tele-health data is not robust enough* to commit to investment, that would accelerate or scale this initiative and that was needed through the pandemic. Another senior accountant, wanted to convey the message of **energy** and **curiosity:** *Grab the curiosity around something and drill to the lowest level to understand.* Most of all capability development is essential to really understand what works and who are the winners.

The learning capacity of the workforce was considered a key factor with all workforce and stakeholders deemed to need skill building, particularly in digital health. While VBHC was not necessarily at the forefront of health agendas, the notion of value-based health and health outcomes was indicated in all interviews and goals around performance metrics. It was clear that technology was at the forefront of anticipated revolutionary change. Interviews did not elaborate on the financial upskilling of clinical staff; however, most interviewees believed that enriched data would foster further insights and need for more knowledge. The areas of workforce upskilling relating to health, digital and financial literacy required for staff working in accounting and hospital administrator roles is indicated in the following subsection.

6.4 Value-Based Impacts

In understanding how accountants can be supportive in the implementation of VBHC, this book culminated in the importance of integrating learning teams to be part of the journey in terms of assessing the workforce impacts around performance evaluation, operational budgeting and capital investment and the important role of digital health that impacted across the healthcare value chain.

In Chapter 2, attention was given to the role of accounting in non-financial performance evaluation for measuring outcomes in VBHC approaches. This chapter was designed to support the upskilling of accountants to be recognised for their ability to weave narratives from the data – both financial and non-financial for measuring outcomes. In Chapter 3, the idea that working to a structured activity-based funding (ABF) model creates a cost-efficiency mindset and does not allow for experimentation. Instead, interviewees suggested the model be considered as a hypothesis to test ideas and experimentation. That is, ABF can be important in value chain cost determination inputs, but not considered adequate to measure or fund VBHC outcomes. The overall budget needs to be reconciled with outcomes.

Strategically minded CEOs and leadership highlight the strategic investment-centre mentality that fosters change in this sector. In addition, insights from Finland provided progressive activity that can be part of continued research to determine whether restructuring the sector according to a combined primary, social and hospital jurisdictional budget works to effect desired VBHC outcomes. Chapters 4 and 5 highlight the importance of being engaged in digital health investments and enhancing the workforce capacity. The presence of distinct silos of expertise within organizations underscores the necessity for a collective upskilling of the workforce. This initiative aims to enhance the comprehensive understanding of the support function and its potential when leveraged through co-production. Such a strategic approach to skill development is imperative for fostering collaborative efforts and breaking down knowledge barriers, thereby enabling a more integrated and effective working environment.

In summarising, the interviewees confirmed the four important skills that future accountants are expected to have. These are depicted in Table 6.3.

Table 6.3 Important skills for future accountants

Category of skills	*Subcategories of skills*	*Description*
Ethical skills	Technical ethical skills	• Knowledge of the ethical guidelines and code of conduct of accounting professional bodies. • Ability to scrutinise the inputs (e.g., data and algorithms) and outputs (e.g., automated accounting entries and AI-assisted decision-making) to spot unconscious biases and prejudices that can lead to ethical issues.
	Interpersonal ethical skills	• Acting as "critical friend" by asking the right questions when it comes to the quality of data produced and used by digital technology. • Acting as the gatekeeper of corporate data.
Digital skills	Basic digital skills	• Develop and master digital skills with core technologies already adopted at scale (e.g., cloud, standard BI and digitisation of tax returns).
	Advanced digital skills	• Become familiar with newer and more advanced technologies (e.g., AI, blockchain and advanced Business intelligence (BI)).

(*Continued*)

Table 6.3 (Continued)

Category of skills	*Subcategories of skills*	*Description*
	Data skills	• Programming (e.g., from a user perspective, contextualised and broad). • Data management skills (e.g., accuracy, consistency and relevance). • Data analysis (e.g., synthesis of diverse data types and effective presentation).
Business skills	Consulting and business advisory skills	• Act as internal consultants leveraging on the knowledge of the organisation's history and the outputs of digital technology systems. • Ability to facilitate internal collaborations between departments to support data-driven decision-making. Synthesise and communicate various forms of data across the organisation.
	Strategic thinking	• Ability to understand the broader business context and possess vision.
Soft skills	Adaptability	• Ability to stay focused in times of adversity; adaptive thinking; flexibility to adapt in the evolving working environment.
	Communication	• Act as the link between internal and external stakeholders; storytelling for effective communication of complex and diverse data.
	Lifelong approach to continuous personal and professional development (CPD)	• Self-initiative to upskill, unlearn, relearn.
	Critical thinking	• Higher cognitive critical thinking, evaluate uses and limitations of automation, combine and interrogate diverse types of data construct multidimensional narratives.
	Dynamic problem-solving	• Embrace uncertainty; adopt a positive attitude under adversity; explore solutions using evolving assumptions.
	Emotional intelligence	• Be aware of own and others' emotions and how this impact one's reactions; empathy as a key component of liaising with customers and internal stakeholders

Note
Adapted from "Exploring the impact of 4IR on skills and personal qualities for future accountants: A proposed conceptual framework for university accounting education" by Tsiligiris, V., & Bowyer, D., 2021, *Accounting Education*, *30*(6), p. 639 (https://doi.org/10.1080/09639284.2021.1938616). Copyright © 2021 by Taylor & Francis Online.

From a strategic perspective, meeting all these goals will require compromise, and negotiation is an important part of managing compromise. As can be noted throughout this book, the move to VBHC is slow and requires trials to see the impacts across the value chain. Education should concentrate on the holistic outcomes and goals of the VBHC movement, or the quadruple aims, if Australia ultimately prefers to take this position (Tsiligiris & Bowyer, 2021). Ultimately the measure, deliver and pay model captures the essence of change and the role of the accountant in each of these aspects. Table 6.4 presents a range of strategies and values that are in alignment with the objectives of workforce upskilling and the development of hybridized expertise.

Table 6.4 A strategic values-based framework for VBHC implementation: Workforce upskilling

Strategy/Values	*How can accountants support?*
Integrate learning teams	Be part of the journey in terms of assessing workforce impacts, digital health investments and enhancing workforce technological capacity **Assist:** Engage with cross-discipline and cross-functional teams to share strategic insights and build needs analysis around technology-focused upskilling.
Industrial value	Understanding efficiency and standardisation in VBHC decision-making is essential to reducing costs and supporting outcomes. **Assist:** Educate on the reasons for standardised data flows for efficient and secure outcomes. Investigate outliers and provide performance frameworks around these cases.
Market value	Educational offerings are multiplying as digital health technologies expand. **Assist:** Co-create educational solutions with trusted partners to manage overload and ensure systems knowledge as well as detailed.
Domestic value	A detailed skills inventory is required to manage workforce upskilling and determine needs requirements. **Assist:** Create a hierarchy of collegial co-producers to work together in prioritising needs in upskilling the workforce.
Civic value	Ensure governance and regulation is an essential component of workforce upskilling. **Assist:** Identify professional body guidance and use where appropriate for CPD. Determine gaps in educational requirements and inform professional body.
Inspired value	Innovations generate workforce upskilling requirements, just as workforce upskilling calls for innovate delivery methods to manage work-life balance and maintain engagement. **Assist:** Support with value contributions from accounting, that engage others from outside the discipline. Work with clinicians to co-create educational solutions.
Fame value	A well-educated and functioning workforce is recognised globally. **Assist:** Accounting to support profiling initiatives. Engage in cost-benefit modelling and support internal innovations.

6.5 Conclusion

In summary, this chapter contributes a holistic perspective on the workforce's role in the VBHC transition, emphasising the intertwining of digital competencies, ethical responsibilities and collaborative efforts to achieve optimal healthcare outcomes.

1. **Highlighting the Shift to VBHC:** The chapter contributes by providing a thorough analysis of the movement towards VBHC, underscoring its significance in the contemporary healthcare landscape.
2. **Digital Health's Central Role:** This chapter contributes by establishing the centrality of digital health technologies, from data-capturing systems to AI's predictive modelling capabilities, in driving the transition towards VBHC.
3. **Addressing Technological Disparities:** By identifying potential challenges posed by health information technologies, the chapter contributes by bringing forth the importance of bridging technological disparities and strengthening digital health literacy.
4. **Redefining Healthcare Roles:** The chapter illuminates the evolving roles of healthcare professionals, emphasising the need for them to become co-producers using digital health tools and the rise of the patient as an active agent in their own care.
5. **Introduction of Hybridised Skills:** One of the standout contributions is the introduction and elaboration of the concept of hybridised skills. The chapter articulates the necessity for healthcare providers to merge traditional clinical skills with an understanding of digital technologies and data analytics.
6. **Ethical Standards in Accounting:** Drawing upon international ethical standards, the chapter positions the role of accountants within VBHC, emphasising their accountability to act in the public's interest and their expanded role in analysing both financial and non-financial data.
7. **Emphasis on Continuous Upskilling:** The chapter underscores the imperative of ongoing education and upskilling for the entire healthcare workforce. It details the requirements for digital health competencies, AI proficiency and adaptive skills to navigate the evolving VBHC landscape.
8. **Strategic Insights and International Examples:** By integrating insights from strategic perspectives and offering international examples, the chapter offers a well-rounded understanding of the challenges and opportunities in the shift towards VBHC.
9. **Interdisciplinary Collaboration:** The chapter stresses the importance of removing silos and promoting interdisciplinary collaboration, emphasising co-production and collective upskilling across the healthcare value chain.

10 **The Role of Negotiation and Compromise:** Addressing the complexities of the VBHC transition, the chapter delves into the significance of negotiation in managing compromises, ensuring that healthcare outcomes remain at the forefront.

By drawing parallels with the content of previous chapters, this chapter offers a synthesised understanding of the overarching theme of the book, ensuring continuity and comprehensive insight into the role of accounting in the VBHC movement. In conclusion, the following four key takeaways provide the basis for hybridising accounting expertise in the healthcare sector.

Key Takeaway 1: Accountants need skills to act as a **business co-producer** in providing a strong advisory and supporting role in leading innovative change, by recognising trends and opportunities as well as managing risk.

Key Takeaway 2: Accountants need to move more into being a **data navigator and transformer** using analytics and visualisations for strategic deep dives and innovative insights on performance outcomes, for more streamlined efficient operations that extend traditional boundaries.

Key Takeaway 3: While performance reporting is a given requirement, it is argued that digitally enhanced **audit and assurance** will provide greater support to clinical managers, particularly if enhanced with AI.

Key Takeaway 4: A champion for **sustainability** in developing investment appraisal and budgeting frameworks that support the achievement of sustainable development goals from a population health and wellbeing to sustainable resourcing.

References

Busse, T. S., Nitsche, J., Kernebeck, S., Jux, C., Weitz, J., Ehlers, J. P., & Bork, U. (2022). Approaches to improvement of digital health literacy (eHL) in the context of person-centered care. *International Journal of Environmental Research and Public Health*, *19*(14), 8309. 10.3390/ijerph19148309

Hsiao, C. J., Dymek, C., Kim, B., & Russell, B. (2019). Advancing the use of patient-reported outcomes in practice: Understanding challenges, opportunities, and the potential of health information technology. *Quality of Life Research*, *28*(6), 1575–1583. 10.1007/s11136-019-02112-0

International Ethics Standards Board for Accountants. (2022). *Handbook of the international code of ethics for professional accountants, including International Independence Standards (2022 digital ed.)*. International Federation Accountants (IFAC). https://www.ethicsboard.org/

Jarva, E., Mikkonen, K., Andersson, J., Tuomikoski, A. M., Kääriäinen, M., Meriläinen, M., & Oikarinen, A. (2022a). Aspects associated with health care professionals' digital health competence development – A qualitative study. *Finnish Journal of EHealth and EWelfare*, *14*(1), 79–91. 10.23996/fjhw.111771

Jarva, E., Oikarinen, A., Andersson, J., Tuomikoski, A. M., Kääriäinen, M., Meriläinen, M., & Mikkonen, K. (2022b). Healthcare professionals' perceptions of digital health competence: A qualitative descriptive study. *Nursing Open*, *9*(2), 1379–1393. https://doi-org.ezproxy.lib.rmit.edu.au/10.1002/nop2.1184

Konttila, J., Siira, H., Kyngäs, H., Lahtinen, M., Elo, S., Kääriäinen, M., Kaakinen, P., Oikarinen, A., Yamakawa, M., Fukui, S., Utsumi, M., Higami, Y., Higuchi, A., & Mikkonen, K. (2019). Healthcare professionals' competence in digitalisation: A systematic review. *Journal of Clinical Nursing*, *28*(5-6), 745–761. 10.1111/jocn.14710

Russell, R. G., Novak, L. L., Patel, M., Garvey, K. V., Craig, K. J. T., Jackson, G. P., Moore, D., & Miller, B. M. (2022). Competencies for the use of artificial intelligence–based tools by health care professionals. *Academic Medicine*, *98*(3), 348–356. 10.1097/ACM.0000000000004963

Tsiligiris, V., & Bowyer, D. (2021). Exploring the impact of 4IR on skills and personal qualities for future accountants: A proposed conceptual framework for university accounting education. *Accounting Education*, *30*(6), 621–649. 10.1080/09639284.2021.1938616

Vollbrecht, H., Arora, V., Otero, S., Carey, K., Meltzer, D., & Press, V. G. (2020) Evaluating the need to address digital literacy among hospitalized patients: Cross-sectional observational study. *Journal of Medical Internet Research*, *22*(6), e17519. 10.2196/17519

7 VBHC Control, Performance Measurement and Risk Management

Future Research Agenda

Tarek Rana, Gillian Vesty, Miia Jansson, and Kerryn Butler-Henderson

7.1 Introduction

This concluding chapter provides further reflections and extensions on the emergent themes offering future research directions. This chapter also explores new perspectives which were not fully explored in other chapters of the book. The intention is to develop future research scholarship in the context of value-based healthcare (VBHC), investment in digital health, the changing roles for accountants, along with the impacts of technology on management control, performance measuremet and risk management that will inevitably persist for many years to come.

This chapter focuses on the transformative role of digital health technologies in the healthcare sector, primarily within the context of VBHC. As a cornerstone of the ongoing transition towards VBHC, digital health interventions are recalibrating healthcare outcomes by strategically aligning resources to amplify value across the healthcare value chain. Simultaneously, emerging technologies offer promising avenues for enhancing care transitions through advanced systems for capturing and analysing performance data while integrating artificial intelligence (AI) for predictive modelling.

However, these breakthroughs in digital health technology may also accentuate health disparities, especially under circumstances where access to such technology is skewed or comprehension is limited. The COVID-19 pandemic has underscored the essentiality of robust digital health strategies in maintaining efficient healthcare delivery amidst unforeseen challenges. It has also highlighted the significant role of digital health literacy in empowering patients and improving their health outcomes, while spotlighting the imperative need to enhance the digital competency of healthcare providers and their managers.

This chapter explores a few emergent themes such as the role of accountants in a digitally transformed healthcare sector, the ethical obligations of accountants in the changing landscape of management control and risk management in VBHC, including the innovation therein. This chapter delves into how the digitisation of the healthcare sector is redefining the role of accountants,

DOI: 10.4324/9781032685489-7

extending their responsibilities from transaction-oriented tasks to strategic decision-making based on both financial and non-financial data analysis. In light of this evolution, the chapter also revisits the ethical obligations of accountants, underscoring their duty to act in the public interest.

Moreover, in this chapter we probe into the challenges presented by the implementation of VBHC for risk management. The concept of VBHC has presented a new set of complexities for risk management, owing to the potential influence of multiple factors on health outcomes, cost-efficiency and patient satisfaction. Consequently, we propose that VBHC risk management frameworks should be viewed through the lens of innovation in order to effectively manage risks and uncertainties, especially within the context of public healthcare. This chapter examines these interconnected emergent themes, shedding light on how to successfully navigate this digital transformation journey with an emphasis on improved healthcare outcomes.

7.2 Emergent Themes for Future Research

7.2.1 Digital Health Transition in Healthcare Sector

This theme focuses on the role of digital health technologies and their impact on the healthcare sector, particularly in the context of VBHC. Digital health interventions are pivotal in the transformation towards VBHC, which aims to optimise health outcomes by aligning resources to maximise value across the healthcare value chain.

Emerging technologies have the potential to enhance healthcare transitions, providing advanced systems for capturing and analysing performance data, including predictive modelling with AI. However, the same technologies might exacerbate health disparities, especially in scenarios where technological access is one-sided or limited in comprehension.

The COVID-19 pandemic underscored the need for robust digital health strategies, as it led to unprecedented challenges in maintaining efficient healthcare delivery. This situation emphasised the significance of effective digital health literacy to empower patients and improve their health outcomes. Simultaneously, there is a need to improve the digital competency of managers in healthcare providers so they can effectively guide patients in navigating these digital platforms.

7.2.2 The Role of Accountants in a Digitally Transformed Healthcare Sector

With the advent of digitalisation in healthcare, the role of accountants in the healthcare sector is evolving. Traditionally, their tasks were mostly transaction-oriented and focused on data entry and reporting. However, the changing landscape demands that accountants extend their data skillset beyond collecting and processing numerical or finnacial data. They need to understand the broader implications of the variety of sources data they could work with and the economic and social factors that affect the healthcare institutions they serve.

With the aim to transition towards VBHC, there is a growing need for accountants to develop critical analytical skills to identify and process both financial and non-financial data in both strcutured and un-structured form from traditional and contemprorary sources. This approach aids in understanding value outcomes and budgetary pressures, crucial for strategic decision-making and enhancing overall healthcare outcomes.

Digital health technologies also necessitate accountants to adapt their theories and practices, particularly around performance measurement, operational budgeting and capital investment. Accountants must understand the emerging technologies' dynamics and their impact on the healthcare value chain. For instance, the telehealth data during the pandemic was not robust enough to commit to investments that would accelerate or scale the care initiative, reflecting the need for more comprehensive digital health competencies among healthcare accountants.

7.2.3 Revisiting the Ethical Obligations of Accountants

The evolving role of accountants in the healthcare sector also underscores the importance of their professional and ethical obligations. The International Ethical Accounting Standards Board (IESBA) Code of Ethics explicitly states the responsibility of professional accountants to act in the public interest, satisfying the needs beyond an individual client or organisation.

The VBHC model also emphasises the need for accountants to uphold these ethical standards. They are expected to align their professional services with the overarching goal of maximising health outcomes across the healthcare value chain. This role expansion means accountants need to have a better understanding of the non-financial performance measures associated with VBHC, moving beyond the conventional model of cost-efficiency or health system efficiency.

Given these new dynamics, it is imperative that accountants adapt to these changes, upskill where necessary and contribute more proactively and strategically to decision-making processes. This adjustment will involve understanding data-driven insights and narratives, learning to negotiate value and discerning where strategic disinvestments and reinvestments need to occur. The evolving role of accountants in the healthcare sector forms an integral part of the larger digital transformation journey, with the goal of improved healthcare outcomes.

7.2.4 VBHC Risk Management

The concept of VBHC presents significant challenges for risk management, as its implementation and execution can be affected by several factors, influencing health outcomes, cost-efficiency, health system efficiency and patient satisfaction. VBHC risk management has become increasingly important in recent years as the push towards more patient-centred, outcome-focused care models becomes more pronounced for cost-effective models. However, the COVID-19 pandemic has created additional challenges for VBHC risk management as healthcare providers strive to balance the need for patient-centric care with the immediate demands of the pandemic. Thus, the COVID-19 pandemic and VBHC are two global challenges that have recently captured the world's attention. COVID-19 has caused widespread illness, death and significant disruption in healthcare delivery, while the transition to VBHC is causing shifts in traditional healthcare practices, systems and models. We argue that, while the COVID-19 pandemic presents a danger, healthcare providers need to learn how both providers and care receivers benefit from a VBHC approach to enhance risk management in the healthcare value chain. We must use Management Control Systems (MCS) effectively to manage the risk of both the pandemic and the transition to VBHC to achieve long-term sustainability in healthcare value chain.

While the two issues are fundamentally different, some meaningful connections between them are more visible through the MCS and risk management lens. One key role of MCS in managing VBHC risks is to enable healthcare providers to identify and assess VBHC risks. Effective risk identification and assessment requires a comprehensive approach that includes the identification of VBHC risks, the assessment of the potential impacts of these risks and the development of strategies to mitigate these risks. MCS can help healthcare providers identify and assess VBHC risks by providing a framework for risk identification and assessment and tools for data analysis and modelling. Effective monitoring and reporting are critical roles of MCS that helps in managing VBHC risks. It requires the development of appropriate performance metrics, as well as the implementation of controls to ensure the accuracy and reliability of healthcare data. By implementing MCS and improving performance, healthcare providers can reduce risk of adverse events and negative implications. In this way, MCS can help healthcare providers monitor and report VBHC risks by providing a framework for performance measurement and reporting and facilitating data analytics to make informed decisions for risk management.

VBHC presents a range of risks to healthcare providers, including risks related to care quality, patient satisfaction, resource allocation and healthcare costs. On the issue of risk and uncertainty, transitioning to a VBHC model involves multiple interconnected factors such as changing healthcare policies, increasing patient expectations, the evolving role of technology in healthcare and the need for cost-effective care. These factors interact in complex ways, and their timing and effects are difficult to predict with certainty. As a result, a high degree of uncertainty is associated with VBHC, making it difficult to plan and prepare for potential risks where risk management can play a critical role.

Global VBHC risks can have cascading effects across multiple sectors of the healthcare system. This makes it difficult to isolate and systematically manage individual risks. These challenges are compounded by access to reliable data and information, which may be limited or incomplete in some regions or sectors. This can make it difficult to assess and manage VBHC risks effectively.

VBHC risk management is also influenced by insitutional, political and social factors such as competing priorities, multiple and sometimes conflicting stakeholder interests and institutional barriers. These factors can complicate efforts to address VBHC risks in a coordinated and effective manner. To this end, addressing these challenges will require a coordinated and collaborative effort across sectors and stakeholders and a commitment to ongoing monitoring and adaptation in the face of changing healthcare needs and expectations. Healthcare providers that can manage VBHC risks effectively will be better positioned to achieve long-term sustainability and resilience in the face of an uncertain and rapidly changing healthcare environment.

7.2.5 Risk Management Innovation in VBHC

Let us consider the management of VBHC risk in the context of the public healthcare sector. Being a complex and dynamic process, the transition to VBHC poses significant challenges for risk management within the public healthcare.

The concept of innovation has diverse interpretations. Nonetheless, a common understanding suggests it is about creating and actualising novel concepts. In the healthcare context, specifically VBHC, innovation means devising new or enhanced services, procedures or protocols that add value and propel transformation. It encompasses harnessing creativity and assimilating novel knowledge, technologies and methodologies to address pre-existing issues or uncover fresh opportunities.

Future research can utilise uncertainty principle to explore the interplay between project uncertainty, healthcare strategy and MCS. The findings of this book postulates that project uncertainty is a critical determinant of healthcare strategy and the design of MCS. In such unpredictable conditions, healthcare systems must adopt flexible strategies and MCS that can adjust to changing circumstances and respond to unexpected challenges. The findings and discusisons of this book further establishes a positive relationship between project uncertainty and the adoption of adaptable healthcare strategies and MCS, which allow for experimentation, feedback and learning.

The influence of MCS on healthcare performance is reliant on the degree of uncertainty within the project environment. Flexible MCS that encourage experimentation, feedback and learning are associated with superior healthcare performance in uncertain environments. Yet, in more specific circumstances, more rigid MCS emphasising compliance and standardisation may prove more effective. However, this remains an under-researched research domain particuarly within the context of public-sector health service delivery.

Unlike private or commercial entities, public-sector healthcare domain must prioritise community or population health and welfare over economic profit generation. Innovation can help public organisations develop and/or enhance processes to deliver healthcare services more efficiently and effectively, thereby boosting community health outcomes. Also, being under government supervision and demands for public accountability, public service organisations are subject to higher standards of control and performance monitoring by citizens, elected officials and stakeholders. Emphasising innovation can assist public-sector healthcare organisations in demonstrating their commitment to service improvement across healthcare value chain, leading to better citizen outcomes and more effective engagement with risk and uncertainty.

Thus, innovation is crucial in managing public-sector healthcare services. Primarily, as societal health needs evolve, the public health sector must adapt to meet these new demands. Furthermore, facing budgetary constraints, innovation can lead to greater efficiency in reducing costs, enhancing processes and achieving intended outcomes. Finally, public service organisations must interact with citizens to understand their healthcare needs, thereby building trust and support for better healthcare services. Innovation can enhance health service performance and citizen engagement using new technologies and platforms, like social media and online citizen forums.

7.3 Directions for Future Research

7.3.1 Hybridised Skills Requirements

Based on this theme some potential directions for future research are discussed:

- Role of Accountants in VBHC: As the role of healthcare providers continues to evolve with technology, there is a need for more research on the changing role of accountants within VBHC, specifically, how accountants can best support healthcare providers and administrators in their transition towards a VBHC model.
- AI and Data Analytics in Healthcare Accounting: With the advancements in AI, ML and data analytics, future research should explore the implications and opportunities these technologies offer within the healthcare accounting and management domain. Understanding the algorithms, biases and ethical considerations associated with AI and ML can provide valuable insights and strategies for managing skills requirement of accountants for improving healthcare outcomes.
- Training and Education for Digital Health Competencies: The rapid integration of digital technologies in healthcare necessitates a comprehensive understanding of digital health skills and competencies. Future research could focus on the most effective methods of training and education for healthcare providers and administrators as well as accountants to acquire these competencies.

- Impact of Personal Attributes and Organisational Factors on Digital Health Competencies: An exploration of how personal attributes (such as willingness, ability and confidence) and organisational factors (like job position, changing healthcare practices, collegial, managerial and technical support) influence the acquisition and implementation of digital health competencies of accountants can provide valuable insights for healthcare organisations.
- Risk Management in AI and Digital Health Solutions: As AI becomes increasingly integrated into healthcare, more research should be conducted on risk management associated with AI and digital health solutions. Understanding the potential risks and developing robust strategies to mitigate them will be critical for the safe and effective use of these technologies in healthcare organisations.
- AI-Related Clinical Competencies: Future research could focus on the necessary AI-related clinical competencies for healthcare providers and their managers. These competencies will be critical for effective utilisation and integration of AI in healthcare practices.
- Cost-Benefit Analysis of AI in Healthcare: As AI and digital health technologies are becoming increasingly prevalent in the healthcare field, more research is needed to understand the cost-benefit analysis of implementing these solutions. Accountants always play a critical role in providing this cost-benefit analysis.
- The Integration of Clinical and Accounting Perspectives in Healthcare: More research is needed on how to best align or integrate clinical and accounting perspectives within healthcare organisations, particularly within the context of VBHC. This could lead to more holistic strategies for improving organisational efficiency and patient outcomes.
- Ethical Standards for Accountants in Healthcare: Given the specific ethical considerations in the healthcare field, more research should be conducted into the appropriate ethical guidelines for accountants working within healthcare organisations.
- Role of Professional Accounting Organisations in VBHC: Future research could examine the role that professional accounting organisations, such as the CPA Australia, International Federation of Accountants and IESBA, can play in promoting and supporting the transition to VBHC.

7.3.2 *Strategic Support Service Provision: Changing Role of Accounting*

Based on this theme, the following are some potential directions for future research:

- Role of Technology in Accounting: As technology continues to revolutionise healthcare, accounting and management research should examine its influence on the accounting practices within healthcare organisations and within healthcare supply chain.

- Performance Metrics in VBHC: More research is needed to understand how performance metrics and measurements are being designed and implemented within the context of VBHC.
- Financial Literacy of Clinical Staff: While this area was not specifically highlighted in this study, it may be valuable to explore the role of accounting or financial literacy among clinical staff and how it influences their decision-making and healthcare outcomes.
- Role of Non-financial Data in Healthcare Accounting: Future research could investigate the role of qualitative and non-financial data in healthcare accounting, how it can be integrated with financial data and its impact on VBHC decision-making.
- Healthcare Budgeting and Cost Management: As the role of healthcare accountants is shifting, research could investigate the challenges and solutions in managing healthcare budgets, managing costs and resource allocation, especially in a VBHC setting.
- Value Analytics in Healthcare Accounting: Research could further explore the concept of value analysis in VBHC accounting, focusing on how prospective value analysis can influence budgetary and resource allocation decisions and both financial and non-financial outcomes in VBHC.
- Changing Role of Accountants in Healthcare: With the changing landscape of healthcare, the role of accountants in this sector is also changing. Future research could delve deeper into this shift from transactional roles to more strategic roles and analytical roles, determining how this shift is impacting and will be impacting healthcare outcomes and effectiveness.
- Development of Analytical Skills in Healthcare Accountants: As accountants need to look beyond just financial numbers and establish relationships among accounting and healthcare professionals, future research should explore the type of strategic and analytical skills required for accountants in healthcare and effective ways to foster collaborationskills.
- Negotiation Skills in Healthcare Accounting: As preparing budgets and resources allocation becomes increasingly important in contemporary business environment, research should explore the role of negotiation skills in VBHC accounting. This includes determining the value of certain services or initiatives or strategies and deciding where to allocate or not-to-allocate resources.
- Data Robustness and Decision-making: There is a need for research to investigate the relationship between data robustness and decision-making in VBHC accounting. This includes understanding the exogenous and endogenous factors that determine the robustness of data and how it influences investment decisions. Moreover, how these exogenous and endogenous factors affect the social impact of VBHC decision-making of healthcare projects. VBHC projects, particularly when aiming at social impact, are usually the function of social and institutional context and values. In addition, how the dimensions of social externalities facilitate or hinders the accounting measurability of impact from VBHC warrants further research.

- Impact of Telehealth and Investment Decisions: Future accounting and business research could specifically focus on telehealth, which is going through rapid transformation due to advances in AI, evaluating its strength in data processing, robustness and the impact it has on accounting information for investment decisions within healthcare organisations.
- Workforce Upskilling in Healthcare: Research should explore the different areas where workforce upskilling is required, such as digital health and financial literacy. This could include developing effective strategies for upskilling and evaluating the impact of these strategies on VBHC outcomes.
- Learning Capacity in Healthcare Workforce: Research could explore how the learning capacity of the workforce affects the uptake of new skills and practices, particularly in relation to digital health and financial literacy.

7.3.3 Value-Based Impact

Based on this theme, the following are some potential directions for future research:

- Role of Accountants in Non-Financial Performance Evaluation: Research could focus on developing methodologies for non-financial performance evaluation in VBHC, emphasising the role of management accountants in this process. This could involve identifying relevant non-financial data and determining how it could be utilised to measure VBHC outcomes effectively.
- Accounting and Experimentation in Activity-based Funding (ABF) Models: Future studies could explore how the ABF model can be adjusted to promote experimentation and various hypothesis testing in VBHC. This research could consider the potential impacts on cost-efficiency, cost-effectiveness and VBHC outcomes.
- Impact of Strategic Investment-Centre Mentality in Healthcare: Research could investigate how a strategic investment-centre mentality among healthcare management or leadership influences the implementation of VBHC. This could include examining the role of accountants in fostering this mindset using budgets, performance measurements and risk management tools in strategic purposes.
- Effects of Primary, Social and Hospital Jurisdictional Budgeting on VBHC: Future research could study the Australian-Finnish and Australia-other country comparative model of restructuring the healthcare sector budgeting system and its effects on VBHC outcomes. This research could provide insights on how to improve budgeting systems in other countries as well as globally.
- Identifying Key Skills for Future Accountants in VBHC: Studies should identify and categorise the key skills (ethical, digital, business and soft skills) that future accountants would need to effectively support VBHC. This could include developing strategies for fostering these skills in the professional accountancy curriculum and professional development courses.

- Educational Focus on VBHC Outcomes and Goals: Future research should consider how educational programmes can better focus on the holistic outcomes and goals of VBHC, specifically how universities can prepare accountants for their evolving roles.
- Accountant's Role in the Measure, Deliver and Pay Model: Research could investigate the evolving role of accountants in the measure, deliver and pay model within VBHC. This could involve studying the accountant's role in each aspect of this model.
- Integration of Learning Teams in Healthcare: Future studies could explore the effectiveness of integrating learning teams in healthcare settings and their impact on the implementation of VBHC.
- Understanding and Increasing the Value of Healthcare: Research could look at various aspects of value (industrial, market, domestic, civic, inspired and fame) within healthcare and how accountants can contribute to increasing these values in the context of VBHC.

7.3.4 VBHC Risk Management

Based on this theme, following are some potential directions for future research:

- Understanding and Assessing Risks in VBHC Implementation: The transition to VBHC represents a significant paradigm shift in the healthcare sector, necessitating a comprehensive understanding and assessment of the associated risks. The core premise of VBHC is to prioritize patient outcomes in healthcare delivery, aligning incentives with the quality rather than the quantity of care. This approach, while promising, introduces several complexities, challenges and risks that must be meticulously evaluated. As healthcare providers shift focus to outcome-based approaches, there is a potential risk of compromising on certain aspects of care quality that are not directly tied to patient outcomes but are still crucial for holistic care. Detailed research into identifying, categorising and assessing various risks associated with the transition to VBHC can be instrumental. This includes studying the risk of maintaining care quality, ensuring patient satisfaction and managing healthcare costs while moving towards a VBHC model.
- MCS for VBHC Risk Management: MCS play a pivotal role in facilitating the effective transition to VBHC, particularly in managing associated risks. The dynamic nature of healthcare delivery under VBHC requires a robust and adaptive MCS framework. Future research in this domain could significantly contribute to both theoretical advancements and practical applications in healthcare management. Future research can focus on evaluating existing MCS's design and effectiveness in managing VBHC risks and suggesting improvements. This could also involve developing new MCS models specifically tailored for VBHC risk management.

- VBHC Risk Management Amid Uncertainty: In the context of VBHC, managing risks amid high uncertainty is a critical challenge. Uncertainty in healthcare can stem from various sources, including regulatory changes, technological advancements, patient behavior, and public health dynamics. Effective risk management in such a scenario requires a multifaceted approach that combines strategic foresight, robust modelling, and adaptive planning. Research in this area can provide valuable insights and tools for healthcare organizations navigating these complexities. Researching strategies and tools for effectively managing VBHC risks amid high uncertainty could be beneficial. This may include scenario planning, risk modelling and stress-testing VBHC implementations. Research can focus on developing a range of plausible future scenarios in the healthcare context. These scenarios could consider factors like technological disruptions, policy changes, epidemiological trends, and economic shifts. Analyzing the impact of these scenarios on VBHC implementation helps in understanding potential challenges and opportunities. This could involve studying the effects on patient outcomes, cost structures, and care delivery models. Based on these scenarios, research can aid in formulating flexible strategies that enable healthcare organizations to adapt to various future states, ensuring sustained commitment to VBHC principles.
- VBHC Risk Management in Global Healthcare Systems: Given the potential cascading effects of VBHC risks across multiple sectors of the healthcare system, research could focus on devising strategies to manage VBHC risks at a global or system-wide level. This can be achieved through comparative studies of various healthcare systems from various contexts and their approaches to VBHC implementation and risk management. Employing simulation techniques to stress-test VBHC models under extreme conditions. This could involve creating hypothetical extreme market conditions, patient influx scenarios, or regulatory changes to test the resilience of VBHC implementations.
- Addressing Political and Social Factors in VBHC Risk Management: Future studies can focus on understanding how political and social factors affect VBHC risk management. This could involve developing strategies to address these factors effectively, such as facilitating stakeholder dialogue and overcoming institutional barriers to VBHC implementation.
- Role of Data and Information in VBHC Risk Management: Utilizing big data and ML techniques to predict risk patterns and trends. For instance, predictive models can forecast patient outcomes based on various VBHC interventions, helping in preemptive risk mitigation. Research could investigate the challenges related to data access and reliability in VBHC risk management. Future studies can also explore ways to improve data access, storage, quality, privacy, security and use in risk management in a VBHC context.
- VBHC Risk Management in the Public Healthcare Sector: Considering the unique challenges of the public healthcare sector, future research could

focus on developing and testing strategies for VBHC risk management specifically within this sector.

- Impacts of the COVID-19 Pandemic on VBHC Risk Management: The pandemic has brought additional challenges and risks for VBHC implementation. Future research could analyse these challenges and devise strategies for managing them effectively. This could also involve examining the lessons learned from managing the COVID-19 pandemic and how they can be applied to VBHC risk management.
- Building Resilience in VBHC Implementations: Investigating methods to build resilience within healthcare organisations transitioning to VBHC models could be a significant future research direction. This would include examining how risk management can enhance an organisation's capacity to adapt to shocks and stressors.
- Creating a VBHC Risk Management Framework: One research area could involve the development of a comprehensive risk management framework tailored for VBHC. This would include elements such as risk identification, assessment, mitigation and communication processes.

7.3.5 Digital Health Transition in Healthcare Sector

Based on this theme, following are some potential directions for future research:

- Digital Health and VBHC: The intersection of digital health technologies and VBHC presents a fertile ground for academic research. The rapid advancement in digital health technologies, such as telehealth, electronic health records (EHRs), wearable devices, and AI, offers significant opportunities to enhance the implementation of VBHC. However, these advancements also bring unique challenges that necessitate careful examination. Future research in this area could provide critical insights into optimizing digital health interventions within the VBHC framework, ensuring that technology effectively supports the core objectives of improved patient outcomes and cost-efficiency. Future research could explore how emerging digital health technologies are impacting VBHC implementation. This could include case studies on successful VBHC transitions supported by digital health tools, as well as an analysis of potential pitfalls or challenges in this area.
- AI and Predictive Modelling in Healthcare: A key research direction could be the examination of AI and predictive modelling applications in healthcare, particularly in relation to VBHC. This could involve evaluating the effectiveness of these technologies in predicting patient outcomes, streamlining care processes and optimising resource allocation.
- Digital Health Equity: An important area of research could focus on health disparities exacerbated by digital health transitions. This would include investigating access to digital health technologies across different

demographic groups, evaluating the quality of care delivered via these technologies and exploring solutions to address existing disparities.

- Digital Health Strategies in the Context of Pandemics: Given the significant role of digital health during the COVID-19 pandemic, future research could analyse these strategies' effectiveness and suggest improvements for future pandemic responses. This could also involve assessing how digital health strategies can be integrated into overall pandemic preparedness plans.
- Cybersecurity in Digital Health: As digital health technologies continue to proliferate, cybersecurity threats become increasingly important. Future research could explore the challenges and best practices associated with ensuring cybersecurity in the context of digital health. Examining the risks associated with data privacy and security in the use of digital health technologies. This includes compliance with regulations like HIPAA and GDPR and the ethical considerations of patient data use.
- Integration of Digital Health into Existing Healthcare Systems: Investigating how various digital health tools can be integrated into VBHC models to enhance patient care, improve data collection and analysis, and streamline operations. This includes EHRs, telemedicine, mobile health apps, and AI-driven diagnostic tools. Future research could focus on best practices and challenges associated with integrating digital health technologies into existing healthcare systems, especially in a VBHC context.
- Regulatory and Ethical Considerations in Digital Health: Future research could address regulatory and ethical issues associated with the use of digital health technologies. This could include exploring the ethical implications of AI in healthcare, privacy concerns associated with digital health data and the impact of existing regulations on digital health implementation. Identifying barriers to the adoption of digital health technologies in VBHC, such as resistance to change among healthcare providers, technological literacy among patients, and infrastructure challenges.

7.3.6 *Innovation in VBHC*

Based on this theme here are potential directions for future research:

- Understanding Project Uncertainty in VBHC: The concept of uncertainty in project management within the context of VBHC offers a rich area for academic exploration. VBHC, with its focus on patient outcomes and cost-effectiveness, inherently involves a degree of uncertainty due to its reliance on patient-centric outcomes, evolving healthcare technologies, and fluctuating healthcare policies. Understanding how this uncertainty influences healthcare strategy and the design of MCS is crucial for effective implementation and sustainability of VBHC models. Research in this area could shed light on how healthcare organizations can optimally balance flexibility and rigidity in their control systems to adapt to and mitigate the inherent uncertainties. Future research can examine the uncertainty principle within the VBHC context, focusing on how project uncertainty influences healthcare strategy and MCS design.

- Flexible vs Rigid MCS in Public Healthcare: A significant area for future research would be comparing the effectiveness of flexible and rigid MCS in public healthcare delivery under specific circumstances. This could involve assessing their impact on various health outcomes and operational efficiency. Research could explore how MCS can be designed to be more adaptable, allowing healthcare organizations to quickly respond to unforeseen changes or new information. This might involve dynamic goal-setting, real-time data analysis, and agile project management techniques.
- Innovation Strategies for Risk Management in Public Healthcare: Research could examine different innovative strategies for risk management in public healthcare. This could involve exploring novel technologies, protocols and services aimed at reducing risk and improving value outcomes. Examining how uncertainty affects strategic decision-making in healthcare organizations adopting VBHC. This includes studying the implications for long-term planning, investment decisions, and stakeholder management.
- Role of Innovation in Enhancing Public Accountability and Transparency: Future research could focus on how innovation can enhance transparency and accountability in public-sector healthcare organisations, thereby building trust with the public and stakeholders.
- Citizen Engagement and Innovation in Public Healthcare: A key area for future research would be exploring how innovation can enhance citizen engagement in public healthcare, particularly through digital platforms. The research could focus on effective strategies for obtaining citizen feedback and incorporating it into healthcare delivery.
- Efficiency Improvements through Innovation in VBHC: Future research could explore how innovative practices can lead to greater efficiency in public healthcare systems transitioning to VBHC. This could involve evaluating the impact of specific innovations on cost reduction, process enhancement and health outcomes.
- Adaptable Health Strategies and MCS in Uncertain Environments: Future research could focus on the role of adaptable health strategies and MCS in managing VBHC risks, particularly in uncertain environments. This could involve exploring the conditions under which such strategies and systems are most effective.
- Impact of Innovation on Community Health Outcomes: Future research could assess the direct and indirect impacts of innovation on community health outcomes in the context of VBHC. This could involve exploring various innovative practices and their impact on different population groups.
- Use of Emerging Technologies in Risk Management: Future research could examine the use of emerging technologies, like AI, big data analytics and blockchain, in managing risks associated with the transition to VBHC in public healthcare.

- Barriers to Innovation in Public Healthcare Risk Management: Research could also focus on identifying and overcoming barriers to innovation in risk management within the public healthcare sector. This could include factors like regulatory constraints, resource limitations and resistance to change.

7.4 Values-Based Frameworks and Various Perspectives for Future Research Agendas

The strategic values-based framework presented in Table 7.1 emphasises the multiple values and associated evolving role of accountants in supporting the implementation of VBHC, driving change and delivering value across various dimensions in the healthcare sector. Their roles extend beyond traditional financial management to encompass strategic decision-making, ethical governance and innovation, all critical components in the transition to VBHC.

Table 7.1 A values-based framework from strategic management perspective

Values-based perspectives	*How can accountants' support in strategic management?*
Integrate learning teams	Accountants should participate actively in cross-functional learning teams, contributing their unique expertise to improve overall healthcare outcomes. Through collaboration and shared learning, they can better understand and navigate the implications of shifting to VBHC and the use of digital health technologies. Accountants can provide vital input on cost-efficiency, resource allocation and the financial aspects of risk management.
Industrial value	Accountants have a significant role to play in enhancing the industrial value of the healthcare sector. By leveraging data analytics and understanding the financial impacts of different healthcare interventions, accountants can contribute to decisions that drive industrial efficiency and performance. Their expertise in financial management and understanding of VBHC principles can inform strategic investments in digital health technologies and other innovations.
Market value	Accountants can support the healthcare sector's market value by providing accurate and relevant financial data, supporting decision-making processes for market positioning. By understanding the financial implications of VBHC, accountants can help healthcare providers make strategic decisions that optimise patient outcomes and deliver better value for patients, enhancing the market competitiveness of the institution.

(*Continued*)

Table 7.1 (Continued)

Values-based perspectives	*How can accountants' support in strategic management?*
Domestic value	Accountants can contribute to the domestic value by ensuring that resources are allocated effectively and that healthcare services are provided in a cost-effective manner. Through their role in financial planning and management, accountants can ensure that healthcare institutions provide high-quality care that is accessible and affordable for all patients, contributing to the overall health and well-being of the domestic population.
Civic value	Upholding their professional ethical obligations, accountants contribute to the civic value by acting in the public interest and prioritising the needs of the community above individual organisations. Their role in ensuring the financial sustainability of healthcare institutions allows these institutions to deliver on their civic duty of providing accessible, high-quality healthcare to all citizens.
Inspired value	By embracing innovative strategies and digital technologies, accountants can contribute to the inspired value of healthcare institutions. They can inspire change by supporting the implementation of VBHC, helping healthcare providers transition to new models of care and enabling innovation by supporting investments in digital health technologies and other value-adding innovations.
Fame value	Accountants can enhance the fame value of healthcare institutions by supporting transparency and accountability in healthcare operations. By providing accurate, reliable financial information and contributing to the effective management of resources, accountants can enhance the reputation of healthcare institutions as responsible, value-driven organisations that prioritise patient outcomes.

From a performance measurement perspective, the strategic values of integrating learning teams, industrial value, market value, domestic value, civic value, inspired value and fame value are integral to implementing VBHC. Accountants, in this context, emerge as crucial enablers in measuring and tracking these strategic values. As illustrated in Table 7.2 by deploying suitable metrics and KPIs, they can facilitate continuous improvement in learning teams, ensure high industrial and market value through monitoring operational efficiency and competitive positioning and assess domestic value by measuring accessibility, affordability and patient satisfaction. Further, accountants support the measurement of civic value through community engagement and compliance metrics, inspired value through innovation

Table 7.2 A values-based framework from performance measurement perspective

Values-based perspectives	*How can accountants support in performance measurement?*
Integrate learning teams	Accountants can contribute by measuring the performance of learning teams and offering feedback for continuous improvement. By tracking key performance indicators (KPIs) related to learning and collaboration, accountants can help teams gauge their effectiveness and make necessary adjustments.
Industrial value	Performance metrics that reflect operational efficiency, productivity and quality of care are essential. Accountants can facilitate the monitoring of these metrics, ensuring that healthcare institutions are delivering high industrial value.
Market value	Accountants can assist in assessing market position and competitiveness through financial performance metrics like return on investment, cost per patient and revenue growth rate.
Domestic value	Accountants can measure domestic value through metrics related to access and affordability of care, patient satisfaction and population health outcomes.
Civic value	Measurement of civic value can include metrics like community engagement, societal impact and compliance with ethical and legal standards. Accountants can support these measurements with their expertise.
Inspired value	Accountants can help measure inspired value through metrics related to innovation, such as new services developed, technological advancements adopted, and progress towards VBHC goals.
Fame value	Accountants can contribute to the measurement of fame value through metrics that assess public trust, reputation and transparency.

indices, and fame value by gauging public trust and reputation. Hence, the accountant's role in performance measurement underscores their vital contribution to the strategic value alignment in the healthcare sector's journey towards digitisation and value-optimisation.

The management control perspective as listed in Table 7.3 underscores the role of accountants in the strategic values of integrating learning teams, industrial value, market value, domestic value, civic value, inspired value and fame value in the realm of VBHC. Accountants can facilitate learning teams by implementing control mechanisms that ensure alignment with organisational objectives. They can optimise industrial value through cost, quality and efficiency controls and monitor market value through strategic analyses of market trends and competitor positioning. Accountants can also ensure the maximisation of domestic value by managing resource allocation and compliance with healthcare regulations. Furthermore, they can bolster civic

Table 7.3 A values-based framework from management control perspective

Values-based perspectives	*How can accountants support in management control?*
Integrate learning teams	Accountants can support learning teams by ensuring there are adequate control mechanisms to align team activities with organisational objectives.
Industrial value	Accountants can use control mechanisms to ensure that industrial value is maximised, such as cost controls, quality controls and operational efficiency controls.
Market value	Management control in this aspect can include measures to monitor market trends, competitor analysis and strategic planning for market positioning.
Domestic value	Control measures could include managing resources to ensure accessibility and affordability of care, ensuring compliance with healthcare laws and regulations and performance controls for care delivery.
Civic value	Management control mechanisms that contribute to civic value can include ethical and legal compliance controls and public reporting requirements.
Inspired value	Accountants can support the management control of inspired value by implementing controls around innovation and technology adoption, ensuring alignment with VBHC goals.
Fame value	Accountants can implement and monitor controls related to transparency, accountability and public reporting to enhance an organisation's fame value.

value through ethical and legal compliance controls, support inspired value through innovation and technology adoption controls and enhance fame value by implementing transparency, accountability and public reporting controls. Thus, accountants, through effective management control, play a crucial role in actualising strategic value goals in the transition towards digital and VBHC.

From a risk management perspective presented in Table 7.4, accountants play a critical role in supporting the strategic values of VBHC. When integrating learning teams, they can manage risks such as ineffective communication, knowledge silos and resistance to change. To safeguard industrial value, accountants can help identify and mitigate risks like operational inefficiencies, quality failures and cost overruns. They can also support market value by identifying and mitigating market risks, including shifts in consumer preferences and regulatory changes. To maintain domestic value, accountants can manage risks related to access to care, affordability and population health outcomes. Accountants also contribute to civic value by managing risks that might involve ethical violations, non-compliance and reputational damage. Finally, for inspired value, accountants can help manage risks such as failure to innovate, technological obsolescence and misalignment with VBHC goals. Therefore, accountants' expertise in risk management is instrumental in supporting the strategic values of VBHC.

Table 7.4 A values-based framework from risk management perspective

Values-based perspectives	*How can accountants support in risk management?*
Integrate learning teams	Accountants can identify and manage risks related to team learning and collaboration, such as ineffective communication, knowledge silos and resistance to change.
Industrial value	Risks that could compromise industrial value include operational inefficiencies, quality failures and cost overruns. Accountants can help identify, assess and mitigate these risks.
Market value	Accountants can support the identification and mitigation of market risks, such as shifts in consumer preferences, increased competition and regulatory changes.
Domestic value	Accountants can help manage risks related to the delivery of domestic value, such as access to care, affordability and population health outcomes.
Civic value	Accountants can contribute to the management of risks that could compromise civic value, such as ethical violations, non-compliance with laws and regulations and reputational damage.
Inspired value	Risks that could compromise inspired value include failure to innovate, technological obsolescence and misalignment with VBHC goals. Accountants can help manage these risks.
Fame value	Accountants can contribute to the risk management of fame value through risk metrics that assess public trust, reputation and transparency.

From a healthcare supply chain management perspective depicted in Table 7.5, accountants play a significant role in promoting various strategic values. For integrating learning teams, they facilitate cross-functional collaboration, enabling efficient forecasting, procurement and cost reduction. To enhance industrial value, accountants optimise the supply chain, curb waste and improve operational efficiency, ensuring effective inventory management for better patient care. They contribute to market value by identifying supply chain efficiencies that boost financial performance and patient satisfaction. When focusing on domestic value, accountants promote local sourcing, improving community health outcomes and supporting local economies. Accountants bolster civic value by ensuring ethical and sustainable supply chain practices, encompassing fair labour, environmental sustainability and regulatory compliance. For inspired value, they support the use of innovative digital technologies for supply chain management. Finally, for fame value, accountants ensure transparency in procurement and supply chain operations to build public trust and enhance organisational reputation.

In the context of investment in healthcare, as outlined in Table 7.6, accountants play a vital role in fostering a learning culture and aligning teams with investment strategies, contributing to integrated learning teams.

Table 7.5 A values-based framework from healthcare supply chain management perspective

Values-based perspectives	*How can accountants support in healthcare supply chain management?*
Integrate learning teams	Accountants can play a vital role in streamlining the supply chain by fostering cross-functional teams that learn from each other and collaborate effectively. Understanding the intricacies of the supply chain will allow for more accurate forecasting, improved procurement processes and reduced costs.
Industrial value	Accountants can help increase industrial value by optimising the healthcare supply chain, reducing waste and improving operational efficiency. They can also help manage inventory, reducing stockouts and overstock situations that can impact patient care.
Market value	By identifying supply chain efficiencies, accountants can contribute to an organisation's competitive position in the market. Reducing supply chain costs can improve financial performance and patient satisfaction, enhancing the organisation's market value.
Domestic value	Accountants can ensure that supply chain practices contribute to domestic value by focusing on local sourcing where possible, which can improve community health outcomes and support local economies.
Civic value	Accountants can contribute to civic value by ensuring ethical and sustainable supply chain practices, including fair labour practices, environmental sustainability and compliance with regulations.
Inspired value	Accountants can support innovative supply chain practices, such as the use of digital technologies for supply chain management, contributing to the overall inspired value of the organisation.
Fame value	Transparent and ethical supply chain practices can enhance an organisation's reputation and public trust. Accountants can support these practices by ensuring transparency in procurement and supply chain operations.

They guide investments towards enhancing operational efficiency and care quality, boosting the industrial value. To increase market value, accountants steer investments towards new technologies, services or markets to elevate competitiveness. In terms of domestic value, accountants support investments in community health initiatives, expanding access to care and affordability measures. They also facilitate civic value by directing investments towards public health initiatives, community partnerships and ethical healthcare practices. Accountants promote inspired value by backing investments in innovation, research and development. Finally, for fame value, accountants guide investments towards initiatives that heighten an organisation's

Table 7.6 A values-based framework from investment in healthcare perspective

Values-based perspectives	*How can accountants support investment in healthcare?*
Integrate learning teams	Accountants can support investment decisions by fostering a learning culture, ensuring teams understand investment strategies and align their efforts to support them.
Industrial value	Accountants can help maximise industrial value by guiding investments towards areas that increase operational efficiency and quality of care.
Market value	Accountants can contribute to market value by helping guide investments in new technologies, services or markets that increase competitiveness.
Domestic value	Accountants can support investments that enhance domestic value, such as community health initiatives, expanded access to care or affordability initiatives.
Civic value	Accountants can guide investments in projects that enhance civic value, such as public health initiatives, community partnerships and ethical healthcare practices.
Inspired value	Accountants can support investments in innovation, research and development, contributing to the overall inspired value of the organisation.
Fame value	Accountants can guide investments towards initiatives that enhance an organisation's reputation and public trust, such as transparency initiatives, quality improvement projects and community outreach programs.

reputation and public trust, like transparency initiatives, quality improvement projects and community outreach programs.

7.5 Conclusion

As we conclude this book of digital health technologies and their impact on VBHC, the healthcare landscape is rapidly evolving. The digital transformation journey is reshaping healthcare delivery, making it more efficient, personalised and value-based. Simultaneously, it also underscores the vital need for digital health literacy among patients and digital competency among healthcare providers.

Our examination of the evolving role of accountants in this digitally transformed sector indicates that their responsibilities extend far beyond traditional transaction-oriented tasks. As the healthcare industry continues to transition towards VBHC, accountants must adapt to these changes, enhance their analytical skills and understand the broader implications of the data they work with. Their professional services must align with the overarching goal of maximising health outcomes across the healthcare value chain.

The ethical obligations of accountants, as delineated by the IESBA Code of Ethics, emphasise their responsibility to act in the public interest. In the context of the evolving healthcare sector, there is an opportunity for healthcare managers' adherence to equivalent ethical standards is more significant and important than ever. With their expanded role in the VBHC model, accountants and healthcare managers must adapt to the new dynamics, upgrade their skills where necessary and contribute strategically to the decision-making process for long-term social impact.

As we have illustrated, VBHC implementation presents numerous challenges for managers in terms of management control, performance measurement and risk management. The transition towards patient-centred, outcome-focused care models is fraught with risks associated with healthcare quality, patient satisfaction, resource allocation and cost-effectiveness. Successfully managing these risks involves identifying, assessing and developing strategies to mitigate them. Moreover, healthcare providers must balance patient-centric care with the immediate demands imposed by global challenges such as the COVID-19 pandemic.

Finally, managing strategic and operational risks in the context of VBHC requires innovation. Specifically, the public healthcare sector must harness creativity and novel methodologies to improve services and processes, fostering better health outcomes and more efficient healthcare delivery. Innovation in this space will help public organisations meet evolving societal health needs, build trust and enhance citizen engagement. To this end, the intertwining threads of digital health technologies, the evolving role of accountants, ethical considerations and innovative risk management form the fabric of a digitally transformed healthcare sector. As we navigate this transformation, continuous learning, adaptation and innovation will be the guiding principles leading us towards improved healthcare outcomes.

In summary, this chapter offers several contributions by providing in-depth understanding of the challenges and opportunities presented by the digital transformation of the healthcare sector, specifically within the VBHC context. It also sets the direction for future research, underlining the importance of innovation, adaptability and ethical considerations in ensuring improved healthcare outcomes.

1. **Digital Health Transition Contextualisation:** The chapter effectively underlines the instrumental role of digital health interventions, especially within the ambit of VBHC. It provides a comprehensive understanding of the transformative potential of digital health technologies and their strategic importance in amplifying value across the healthcare supply chain.
2. **Highlighting Digital Health Disparities:** By acknowledging the potential risk of increased health disparities due to uneven technology access and understanding, the chapter encourages stakeholders to address these imbalances, thereby ensuring more equitable and accountable health outcomes.

3 **COVID-19's Role in Digital Health Evolution:** The chapter provides a nuanced examination of the COVID-19 pandemic's influence on healthcare delivery, emphasising the significance of digital health literacy and the necessity for enhanced digital competence among healthcare providers to tackle future pandemics.
4 **Accounting Professionals' Role Evolution:** One of the contributions is the delineation of the changing responsibilities of accountants in a digitally transformed healthcare sector. The chapter brings to light the transition from transaction-oriented tasks to strategic decision-making based on comprehensive data analysis where accountants can play vital roles.
5 **Ethical Obligations Revisited:** By revisiting the ethical obligations of accountants in the evolving landscape, the chapter stresses the importance of upholding public interest and aligning with the overarching goals of VBHC.
6 **In-depth Analysis of VBHC Risk Management:** The chapter offers a thorough exploration of the challenges and intricacies associated with implementing VBHC. It delves into the multifaceted risks that come with the VBHC transition, from care quality and patient satisfaction to resource allocation and healthcare costs.
7 **Risk Management Through Innovation:** A unique contribution lies in the chapter's proposal to view VBHC risk management through an innovative lens. It emphasises the potential benefits of creativity and adaptability in addressing the challenges of a rapidly changing healthcare environment.
8 **Future Research Agenda:** By underscoring emergent themes, the chapter sets the stage for future scholarship, exploring areas such as the impact of digital technologies in healthcare, the evolving role and ethical responsibilities of accountants and the intricate dynamics of VBHC risk management. The chapter acts as a roadmap, directing future research towards areas that promise substantial academic and practical insights.
9 **Public Health Sector Focus:** By concentrating on the public healthcare domain, the chapter spotlights the unique challenges and opportunities presented within this context. It emphasises the need for adaptability, innovation and citizen engagement in ensuring effective risk management and enhanced health outcomes.
10 **Holistic Perspective on MCS:** The chapter presents a comprehensive understanding of the role of MCS in managing VBHC risks, emphasising its significance in risk identification, assessment, monitoring and reporting. It accentuates the importance of flexibility and adaptability of MCS, especially in unpredictable healthcare environments.

In conclusion, the following six key takeaways provide the basis for future research agendas.

Key Takeaway 1: The advent of digital health technologies and investment in healthcare significantly enhance the potential for a shift towards VBHC, offering optimised health outcomes by aligning budgets and resources to maximise value across the healthcare value chain.

Key Takeaway 2: As healthcare transitions to VBHC, the roles of accountants and healthcare managers are evolving to incorporate a greater understanding of broader economic factors, analytical skills to assess financial and non-financial data and proficiency in emerging technologies. Their role is extending beyond traditional transaction-oriented tasks to more strategic and analytical responsibilities.

Key Takeaway 3: The transition to VBHC necessitates accountants to uphold high ethical standards as outlined in the IESBA Code of Ethics. Accountants must align their professional services with the overarching goal of maximising VBHC. In the similar vein, healthcare managers might develop parallel code of ethics for delivering health outcomes across the healthcare value chain.

Key Takeaway 4: The implementation of VBHC presents significant challenges for risk management, influenced by several factors like healthcare quality, patient satisfaction, resource allocation and cost-effectiveness. Effective risk management within VBHC requires comprehensive identification, assessment and mitigation strategies.

Key Takeaway 5: The global challenges imposed by the COVID-19 pandemic underline the need for a balance between patient-centric care and immediate pandemic demands. The pandemic has accentuated the need for robust digital health strategies and the significance of effective digital health literacy.

Key Takeaway 6: Innovation plays a crucial role in managing risks in VBHC, particularly in the public healthcare sector. By creating and actualising novel concepts, healthcare services can be improved, leading to better health outcomes and more effective citizen engagement.

Appendix 1: Interview Questions

Overview

Hybridising of accounting skills with aims to upskill accountants/future accountants (and others) in public hospitals. We aim to do this with a focus on creating four interlinked case studies:

- Accounting changes in public hospitals – activity-based funding (ABF), budgeting and performance evaluation
- Information systems – digital health advances and the move to value-based healthcare
- Supply chain and logistics – resourcing changes to support remote/integrated value-based care; consideration of 'costs of quality' processes and preventative costs through the move to integrated care. Focus on impacts of digital health and long-term pandemic-related change
- Upskilling of the workforce – advancing value-based healthcare

Demographics

- Briefly describe your current role and years of experience in this role.

The following questions relate to different areas of expertise and will be used to support different case studies. Specific questions will be asked of respondents, depending on area of expertise.

Case Study 1: Funding Model Change – Toward Value-Based Healthcare

Accounting-Related Questions

- How are the changing federal activity-based funding (ABF) models, and incentives promoted by IPHA, changing the delivery of services
- Is bundled care creating the need for more focus on 'hospital in the home'?
- What is the process of investment appraisal and investment monitoring? For emerging technologies and innovations? How are they recognised?

- What processes are in place to measure effectiveness (cost-benefit analysis)?
- Are CAPEX/OPEX relationships to funding, and support thereof, changing?
- What do you think of the current use of HIS and digital technologies serving our healthcare system?
- How has the HIS system offered better value care? How can it be further improved for better value-based care?
- Do we need new policies and standards to improve the current system to offer better value-based healthcare? Why? What are the current challenges, and how can we overcome them?
- How has digital transformation improved your care in and out of the hospital?
- Has costing changed in the context of moving towards VBHC?
- To what extent/how do patients participate in the development of value-based performance metrics?
- To what extent/how does the hospital governance model foster a culture of trust and collaboration among professionals? How is the value of interdependence in achieving health outcomes managed?
- To what extent/how is the voice of community agents (patient associations, business, institutions, etc.) integrated into the innovation and improvement processes?

Case Study 2: Digital Health, Health Information Systems and Digital Health Interventions

Health Information Systems and Health Information Management (HIS/HIM)

- Do you use any intelligence systems for predictive analytics, forecasting, management of clinical and financial data?
- What are the intelligent systems HIS being used? (i.e., EPIC, CERNER, IBM Cognos, Tableau, Microsoft Power BI, etc?)
- How have you benefited from the use of HIS/digital technologies?
- How does the IT innovation offer better value care for patients (higher quality care with lower cost for gov and patients)?
- Is technology innovation for VBHC activity been actively promoted?
- If so, how is this activity funded (grants, hospital P&L/surplus, industry partners)?
- What is seen as problematic from a user perspective (clinicians/administrators)? System incompatibility – siloed systems within/outside the hospital? Different EMRs/HIS across different major hospitals? System automation (or lack thereof) – for report preparation? Managing legacy systems or training on next-generation solutions?

Case Study 3: Managing the Health Supply Chain in the Digital/ Pandemic Era

Supply-chain Related Questions

- What key services provided by your hospital have been/will be (permanently) impacted by digital health and/or the pandemic era? Are there process maps associated with these changing services that you can share with us?
- Considering 'hospital in the home' and 'hospital without walls' concepts, is value measured in terms of keeping patients out of hospital?
- How is procurement managed in these settings? Is the demand for virtual monitoring/care increasing as hospitals become increasingly bedlocked?
- Are quality costs measured in terms of resourcing changes? To what extent are you investing in care that avoids patient admissions, such as through telehealth, remote digital monitoring and partnership arrangements?
- What are the significant issues faced in terms of managing logistics for remote care?

Case Study 4: Workforce Upskilling for Enhanced Budgeting, Performance Evaluation and Investment Appraisal across the Hospital Value Chain

- Is the 'learning capacity of the workforce' considered a key factor in the organisation?
- How does the organisation upskill staff health and digital literacy?
- Do staff have a good understanding of ABF? Of value-based health?
- How does the organisation upskill staff financial literacy?
- How does the organisation support patient financial literacy, such as understanding how their care is funded as an inpatient or an outpatient or in the emergency department?
- What areas of workforce upskilling relating to health, digital and financial literacy are required for staff working in accounting and hospital administrator roles?

Closing: Are there any further questions we did not ask that you would think relevant to our study?

Index

Index

Note: **Bold** page numbers refer to tables and *italic* page numbers refer to figures.